Physical Education for
the Severely Handicapped

D0861569

Physical Education for the Severely Handicapped

A Systematic Approach to a Data Based Gymnasium

John M. Dunn
James W. Morehouse, Jr.

Oregon State University
Corvallis, Oregon

H. D. Bud Fredericks

Teaching Research
Monmouth, Oregon

5341 Industrial Oaks Blvd.
Austin, Texas 78735

Portions of this book first appeared in *A Data Based Gymnasium* by
John M. Dunn, James W. Morehouse, Jr., Roy B. Anderson, H. D.
Bud Fredericks, Victor L. Baldwin, F. Lynn Blair, and William
Moore, copyright © 1980 by Instructional Development Corporation.

Library of Congress Cataloging in Publication Data

Dunn, John M.
  Physical Education for the severely handicapped.

  Bibliography: p.
  Includes index.
  1. Physical education for handicapped children –
Study and teaching – United States. 2. Physical
education for handicapped children – Oregon – Case
studies. I. Morehouse, James W., 1943
II. Fredericks, H.D. Bud. III. Title.
GV445.D86 1986   371.9′044   85-3662
ISBN 0-936104-69-4

5341 Industrial Oaks Boulevard
Austin, Texas 78735

10 9 8 7 6 5 4 3 2 1   86 87 88 89 90

Contents

Preface

The purpose of writing this book is to present carefully developed and successfully employed concepts and techniques for teaching the severely handicapped. The material presented has been extensively field tested with youngsters enrolled in model classrooms conducted by Teaching Research in Monmouth, Oregon. In addition, the authors have trained many teachers to utilize the concepts presented here. The success of these teachers and their enthusiastic response to the instructional approach led us to develop this volume and its earlier version, *A Data Based Gymnasium: A Systematic Approach to Physical Education for the Handicapped*. The intent of our effort is to convey as clearly as possible an instructional approach for teaching severely handicapped students. The success of our approach may be attributed to careful attention to critical elements in the learning process. These elements—the cue or command, the behavior to be learned, and the procedure for consequating behavior—are thoroughly discussed and analyzed within this text. A conscientious effort has been made to apply concepts derived from learning theory in a concise and understandable manner.

Throughout the book, the reader is cautioned to utilize our instructional approach in a systematic manner and to analyze student progress carefully. Using a data based approach has led us to believe that changes in an instructional program should be made carefully and with sufficient data on student progress to ensure that the change will hasten the learning process. Severely handicapped students and their teachers must see improvement or soon both will become discouraged and frustrated. Unfortunately, improvement in performance with the severely handicapped is often very slow and frequently difficult to discern without analyzing student performance on a daily basis. Thus throughout the book, we present discussions and examples of data recording and analyses. Because our system emphasizes the importance of parents and volunteers, information concerning how they can be included in the instructional program is also presented.

This book is written from the premise that many teachers are uncertain of what or how to teach the severely handicapped. We hope that our book will be accepted for what we perceive it to be—an effort to share with others an instructional approach we have found successful. We do not suggest, however, that the approach described in this book is the final answer to teaching physical education to the severely handicapped. Clearly, it is not, but it is an important contribution to a field where the amount of printed information is extremely limited.

Acknowledgements

The preparation of this manuscript required the assistance of many individuals. Special thanks is extended to our secretaries, Karen Memminger and Bernie Samples, for their help in typing and proofreading material as it was developed for this text. Donald Hammill and his associates at PRO-ED are also to be commended for their willingness to undertake the publication of a text which is new and needed, but in a field with a limited market. We appreciate the publisher's confidence that physical education is important for the severely handicapped and as such deserves published materials to assist others to develop appropriate programs.

The staff of Teaching Research deserves special mention for their willingness to allow us to implement physical education programs with severely handicapped students enrolled in their demonstration classrooms. Without the cooperation of Teaching Research and its director, Dr. Vic Baldwin, the material described in this book would not have developed. The authors acknowledge that the basic concepts described in this book were adapted from Teaching Research's *Data Based Classroom*.

Finally, the authors owe special appreciation to the students on whom our concepts were originally tested. Without their cooperation, effort, and enthusiasm our task would have been impossible. They helped us to recognize the obvious: Physical education instruction must be an integral part of the education of severely handicapped students. We trust that teachers will find our instructional approach helpful in enriching the lives of other severely handicapped individuals.

Overview of the Model 1

Until very recently, the needs of the severely handicapped have not been adequately addressed. Those who deviated significantly from the accepted societal norm were frequently committed to institutions where they were segregated and hidden from the mainstream of public life. Unfortunately, the institutions into which the severely handicapped were placed were usually underfunded and understaffed. This meant that the conditions in many institutions were dehumanizing and without the necessary resources to provide treatment, rehabilitation, and educational programs.

There are signs today, however, that society is becoming more accepting of the severely handicapped as citizens with the same basic needs and rights as all citizens. Within communities, for instance, it is not uncommon now to find group homes and sheltered workshops for those who need guidance and structure in their daily life activities. In recent years, the number of students in public schools with significant impairments has increased dramatically. Many of these students require and are receiving services which some educators felt until very recently were beyond the scope and mission of public education.

Support for the educational rights of the severely handicapped was spearheaded by professional organizations such as the National Association for Retarded Citizens and the American Association on Mental Deficiency. Members from these groups banded together to inform the public that the severely handicapped could benefit from education and training programs. The federal government, too, through the Office of Special Education and Rehabilitative Services (formerly the Bureau of Education for the Handicapped) supported the cause of the severely handicapped by funding projects designed to develop curricular materials and instructional techniques for them. The formation in 1974 of The Association for the Severely Handicapped (TASH) and its rapid membership enrollment attest to the number of professionals and parents committed to improving the educational opportunities available for the handicapped.

The efforts of concerned citizens, parents, and professionals on behalf of the severely handicapped were rewarded in 1975 when P.L. 94-142, The Education for All Handicapped Children Act of 1975, was signed into law by President Gerald R. Ford. This law not only mandated that appropriate educational programs must be provided for all handicapped students, but specified that priority consideration should be given to the severely handicapped and those with unmet needs. P.L. 94-142 also stipulated that the handicapped are to be educated in the least restrictive environment. This implies that placement of severely handicapped children in public schools is the desired goal.

The Education for All Handicapped Children Act of 1975 broadened the traditional concept of special education. Whereas previous views of the term *special education* have spoken to the academic needs of the student, P.L. 92-142 defines special education as including not only traditional classroom instruction but more.

> Special education means specially designed instruction, at no cost to the parents, to meet the unique needs of a handicapped child, including classroom instruction, instruction in physical education, home instruction, and instruction in hospitals and institutions. (*Federal Register*, 1977)

The inclusion of the term *physical education* in the definition indicates clearly that this important service must be provided for the severely handicapped. The goal of this text is to ensure not only that educators recognize this responsibility but to provide information to the teacher so that successful programs can be implemented.

Principles of Program Development

Most educators recognize that structured learning experiences are required to help the severely handicapped benefit from instruction. This means that what is to be taught, how the material is to be presented, why something is taught, and when the skill is to be introduced must be carefully developed and structured by the teacher.

The following are general principles that should be adhered to in the development of quality physical education experiences for the severely handicapped. These concepts were developed after extensive field testing with severely handicapped students enrolled in the National Model Program for Severely Handicapped Children conducted by Teaching Research in Monmouth, Oregon.

1. Every student, regardless of handicapping condition, can learn. This is an important principle that must be continually emphasized in educational programs for the severely handicapped. Occasionally the educational gains may be so small as to appear insignificant, but as long as there is progress the student is benefitting from the program. If the student is not learning, the teacher must experiment by (a) changing methods used to present materials, (b) employing a different technique to reinforce the student, or (c) reducing the task to be learned to smaller steps.
2. Physical education is an integral component of the educational curriculum for severely handicapped students. As such, it is essential that physical education programs adhere to the same standards expected of other areas. Instructional programs should be sequenced, task analyzed, and data based so that performance changes in physical education skills can be determined.
3. Severely handicapped students learn at a slower rate than other handicapped and nonhandicapped students. This means that they will require more extensive and intensive education to compensate for their slower learning rates. Because it is generally impossible to extend the time of the school day, maximum use of the time available will require that parents and volunteers assume responsibility for conducting part of the instruction.
4. There is no way of determining the extent to which a severely handicapped student will progress. Therefore, no ceiling is placed on the physical education curriculum. The teacher must be prepared to take the student as far and as rapidly as possible. Physical education curricular materials should extend from very basic skills, such as executing various body movements while standing, to more advanced skills, such as catching and throwing.
5. Effective instruction for the severely handicapped frequently requires that programs be conducted in a one-to-one relationship. This is necessary because of the heterogeneous nature of the severely handicapped population and the behavior problems sometimes evident with this population. The utilization of trained volunteers is necessary, therefore, to provide individualized instruction in the gymnasium.
6. Physical education experiences for the severely handicapped must be designed to ensure student success. Many severely handicapped students have found previous educational experiences very frustrating. Teachers must be sensitive to this

possibility and the all too common attitude of "I can't." This can best be dealt with by structuring educational experiences in such a way that success is guaranteed.

Defining the Term Severely Handicapped

The basis for the term *severely handicapped* is closely associated with federal law. The Rehabilitation Act of 1973 defines a severely handicapped person as an individual with "a severe disability which seriously limits his functional capacity, who will require multiple vocational rehabilitation services, and who is experiencing substantial functional limitations due to a combination of disabilities" (p. 226). This definition tends to identify the severely handicapped in terms of their employment potential rather than their educational needs. Within the educational literature Sontag, Smith, and Sailor (1977) have explained that the severely handicapped are those whose needs are so great that they are functionally retarded. This phrase emphasizes that severely handicapped students need special assistance to help them function at a level consistent with their ability level. For deaf-blind students this may mean special instruction to help them develop necessary communication skills. Orthopedically handicapped students, unable to stand or sit, will require educational techniques that recognize their mobility limitations. Programs must be developed and instruction individualized to help the severely handicapped overcome, to the greatest extent possible, their functional deficits. The expression *severely handicapped* communicates clearly that these individuals need and will benefit from physical education programs which are well designed and systematically implemented. The intent of the program described in this book is to assist teachers in responding to the physical education needs of low functioning students without concern for the labels assigned to these individuals.

Summary

Within this chapter, a brief introduction to the OSU/TR physical education data based instructional system has been provided. The intent of the program is to provide severely handicapped students with *appropriate* physical education experiences. Emphasis is placed on the importance of individualized and data based instruction. The instructional system may at first seem overwhelming, perhaps not realistic, to educators and administrators who are accustomed to physical education classes of thirty-five or more students. Volunteers, parents, and paraprofessionals are absolutely essential to the management of accountable programs for students with severe learning needs. The physical education environment is not an exception to this rule. In essence, realistic physical education outcomes for severely handicapped students can be achieved only in programs that are individualized and implemented with the assistance of aides and volunteers.

Learning Approach | 2

Oregon State University's Department of Physical Education, in cooperation with the Special Education Department of Teaching Research in Monmouth, Oregon has developed over the past several years a data based physical education program for the severely handicapped (Dunn, Morehouse, Anderson, Fredericks, Baldwin, Blair, & Moore, 1980). The Oregon State University (OSU) Data Based System contains certain elements essential to the instructional model. These address such critical areas as the methods used to present information, reinforcement procedures, curriculum material, management approaches, and personnel needed. In the following paragraphs, some of the ingredients comprising the OSU Data Based System for severely handicapped students will be discussed.

Behavior Modification

The basic approach underlying many effective instructional programs for the moderately and severely handicapped is known as behavior modification. The essence of this approach is that the instructor systematically makes maximal and efficient use of the environment to assist a student in learning a behavior or in extinguishing an undesirable behavior. Behavior modification has three essential elements: (a) the stimulus, also known as the cue, which is the instruction or materials presented to the student; (b) the behavior or task that the student is to learn or do; and (c) the consequence or feedback that the student receives after responding. These elements will be examined repeatedly in relation to their use in the OSU Data Based System.

Cue

The cue is the sign, signal, request, or information that calls for the occurence of a behavior. It is synonymous with the instructions or materials presented to the student. Cues are those things in the environment that set the occasion for the student to behave. For instance, "Johnny, come to me" is a cue for the student to respond to verbal instructions and to move toward the teacher. The presentation of a ball that the student is to throw is a cue. Thus, a cue can take the form of any instructional materials – verbal, printed, or gestural – that are presented to a student. The concept of cue includes all the verbal instructions by the teacher, as well as the gestures and the way objects or materials are presented.

Cues are very important; they represent one-third of the learning model. Most teachers concentrate on cues. The evidence for this is that most teachers have as their primary concern the way in which they present a lesson to the student. Further evidence of the importance of cues is that the building of cues is a major industry within the United States. Educational materials sold by sales people usually can be categorized as cues.

Rules for Appropriate Cueing.   There are some basic rules for appropriate cueing in the *Data Based Gymnasium*. These will be summarized here and discussed more fully in chapter 7, Volunteers: Training and Use.

Each new behavior to be learned by a student will be preceded by a cue. In formal individual instruction, the cue will be specified on the program cover sheet. Its wording should not initially be changed or rearranged since the student's receptive language may be too limited to understand the modified language. The language of cues is important: they should be delivered in a language style that the student is capable of understanding. Ensure that the cue is task specific. For instance, instead of "Gym is now over," a better cue would be "Go shower and dress." The final guideline relative to language is to deliver the cue in command or request form unless one is prepared to give the student an option.

A cue should not be repeated until the student makes a response. (An exception to this is during the correction procedure, when the cue is repeated. This procedure is discussed in Chapter 7.) Repeating cues to students teaches them to respond only to repeated cues. The only time a cue is repeated in this setting is when a student fails to respond or responds incorrectly. At that time, the student is informed that his response is incorrect; the cue is repeated; and the student is assisted in the completion of the task and socially reinforced. This is known as the correction procedure.

The final rule relative to cues is that they should not be weak, a term covering a multitude of potential faults. The cue should not be verbalized in a voice too low to be heard, nor should a cue be delivered without first attracting the attention of the student. Establishing eye contact prior to giving the cue will help ensure the delivery of a strong cue. If total communication is being used with a student, the cue must contain both a verbalization and a manual sign. The absence of either makes the cue weak. The cue must be direct and not offer the student choices. Examples of weak verbal cues include "Would you like to work?," "Time to run around the gym, OK?," "Can you find the basketball?" Instead, the verbal cues should be "It is time to work," "Time to run around the gym," and "Find the basketball."

Behavior

The second major element of this approach is behavior. Behavior is anything a person does, such as lifting a little finger, blinking an eye, kicking a ball, or climbing a rope. In the teaching of students, a behavior is a particular task the student is to learn. It can be something as simple as having students extend their arms or as complex as having them bat a pitched ball.

When teaching a behavior, however, the teacher should constantly keep in mind that most behaviors can be divided into smaller behaviors or pieces of behavior, and it is these pieces of behavior that make up the teaching sequence. Take, for instance, batting a pitched ball. Batting a ball is called a *terminal behavior*, yet it is composed of a number of smaller behaviors—placing each foot in the proper position, grasping the bat with the left hand and the right hand, putting the bat back over the shoulder, fixing the eyes on the pitcher, then following with the eyes the pitched ball, and so on, step by step through the procedure until the ball is batted. The smaller or less difficult behaviors are called *enabling behaviors*, and learning them enables the student to learn the terminal behavior.

Analysis of Behavior.   This process of breaking down a terminal behavior into the enabling behaviors is called analysis of behavior. The physical education teacher is taught to analyze behavior—to break down the behavior to minute sequences and to teach each part as though it were a separate and distinct behavior to be learned. With each new part that is learned, the student must be taught to chain the parts together so they form a smooth-flowing, larger terminal behavior. For a more detailed discussion of analysis of behavior and examples of completed behavior analyses, see Chapter 3.

Enabling behaviors can be chained together either in a forward or backward fashion, and these are logically called forward and reverse chains. A *forward chain* is the sequence of enabling behaviors that make up a terminal behavior and are taught in the order in which they occur. For instance, using a forward chain sequence in teaching a student to walk a balance beam (terminal behavior), a forward chain requires the student to step on the near end of the balance beam and take a prescribed number of steps, and then be helped to step off the balance beam at the other end.

In a *reverse chain* sequence, the student is helped with the beginning of the behavior; in this case she is helped to step up on the balance beam, helped to take the ten steps, and then asked to step off the balance beam independently. When she demonstrates that she can do this task, the student is asked, after being assisted through getting on the balance beam and taking the first nine steps, to take the last step independently and step off the balance beam. After demonstrating this behavior, she is asked to take the last two steps, and so on, until she is performing the entire task independently.

As a general rule of thumb, for motor behaviors the reverse chain sequence is more suitable for the moderately and severely handicapped. One reason for this greater suitability has to do with consequences, for in a reverse chain procedure there is no need to move the consequence from one part of the task to the next since the consequence is always delivered at the completion of the task.

Consequences

Consequences are the third major element of concern and can be likened to a feedback system. After the student performs a particular behavior, feedback or a consequence for that performance is provided. This consequence tells the student that what he or she did was correct or incorrect. In a school setting, one might think of the student taking a motor fitness test and having the test score interpreted as a consequence of the way the individual performed. The consequence can be either pleasing or displeasing to the person receiving it. A consequence that is pleasing to a person is called a *reinforcer*, whereas a consequence that is displeasing is called a *punisher*. The basic concept underlying the delivery of consequences is that the reinforcers delivered following a behavior increase the probability of the behavior occuring again; punishers following a behavior decrease that probability.

Reinforcers. A reinforcer must be pleasurable to the person experiencing it. Because it is pleasurable, and because the person desires that pleasure and associates a particular behavior with the receipt of the reinforcer, a reinforcer by definition increases the probability of a behavior recurring. Students who enjoy social praise may increase the quality or quantity of their performance after being told, "You're doing a nice job!" Consequently, reinforcers by definition must be individualized because what is pleasing and, therefore, reinforcing to one person may not be pleasing and reinforcing to another. The principle of individualization also applies to punishers. A verbal reprimand may be severely punishing (displeasing) to one student whereas another student may not perceive that same reprimand as punishing. Therefore, punishers, like reinforcers, must be individualized.

A basic rule in the use of consequences is to rely, if at all possible, on the natural consequences of the environment. Fortunately, in the physical education environment many activities and experiences are in themselves reinforcing: for example, watching the movement of a ball after it is pushed. For some, however, the natural consequences of the environment are not sufficient and it may be necessary to identify foreign or artificial reinforcers to indicate to the students that their behavior is acceptable.

Reinforcers most frequently used in training programs are categorized as social, tangible, and generalized. *Social reinforcers* include words or physical contact – hugs, squeezes, words of praise or appreciation, letting the student know that his behavior was approved. These are usually considered natural types of consequences that a teacher or parent typically uses. However, we may often exaggerate these social consequences by being more animated or forceful in our delivery of them. We exaggerate them somewhat in order to ensure that the student understands that we strongly approve of his behavior.

Tangible reinforcers include such things as food, water or juice, playing with a toy, time on the playground, watching television – any item or activity the student enjoys. *Generalized reinforcers* are those that can be traded for either a tangible or social reinforcer. A student may be given a token or a point for performance of a behavior. At a specified time, she can trade these tokens or points for such things as food, free time, or social time with a favorite adult. Generalized reinforcers play a major role in our culture. Adults operate on one such token system – money.

Punishers. Punishment is another form of consequence. A punisher is a consequence delivered immediately following a behavior to decrease the probability or the behavior recurring. The word "punishment" is often avoided because of its negative connotation. However, if punishment is defined as a process giving the student feedback that she should not continue a behavior, then it is easy to conclude that punishment is necessary in any effective learning environment. For example, by our definition, saying such things as "No, Sally, throw the ball here" or taking away privileges are possible consequences referrred to as punishers.

The use of both types of feedback, punishers and reinforcers, at appropriate times has been demonstrated as being most efficient. However, the ratio of reinforcers to punishers is also important. Our experience indicates that a ratio of four reinforcers to one punisher delivered to an individual student or to a class as a whole is a minimum acceptable ratio. A ratio less than four to one creates an environment that is aversive to the student who may eventually learn to avoid the learning situation. A low ratio also indicates that the task is probably too difficult for the student, causing her to give incorrect responses. Thus, a low ratio should tell the teacher to simplify the learning task further, perhaps by developing a more detailed task analysis. Most teachers who have adopted the model described herein use a ratio from seven to fifteen reinforcers to each punisher.

Time Out. A third concept that should be discussed under the broad heading of consequences is time out. Technically, time out is considered neither reinforcement nor punishment. The term is a shortened form of "time out from positive reinforcement." However, students who are in a time out condition usually perceive it as punishment, and therefore, operationally it should probably be considered a punisher.

It can be assumed that the gymnasium is typically a reinforcing environment for the student. By the very nature of the activities in the gymnasium and the rewards or consequences the student receives, most enjoy being there. Occasionally, it may be necessary, because of the student's inappropriate behavior, to put him in a time out situation. This means the student temporarily has no opportunity to receive reinforcement. He is essentially ignored or not allowed to participate. Time out is usually administered for only a short period of time. For instance, it has been used successfully for students who begin to "play around" or not attend. It is quite successful with students who are acting out. In a model program, time out has been used successfully by placing the student in an isolated portion of the gymnasium. Only in extreme behavioral disturbances has the student been removed from the gymnasium completely.

Rules for Appropriate Consequating. There are some basic rules for appropriate consequating in the *Data Based Gymnasium*. Again, these will be summarized here and discussed more fully in Chapter 7, Volunteers: Training and Use.

Consequences, whether they be reinforcers or punishers, should be delivered immediately following the behavior. A delay of more than two seconds in the delivery of a consequence is considered too long a time. With severely handicapped students, the more immediate the reinforcer, the more powerful will be its effect. Moreover, if one delays in consequating, a second behavior may be emitted by the student and the consequence, when delivered, may serve to reinforce or punish the second behavior rather than the targeted behavior. For instance, if the cue was, "Jim, throw the ball overhand," and Jim started to throw the ball underhand, the teacher should stop the motor behavior as soon as the incorrect movement is initiated. This allows the student to pair the "no" with the inappropriate arm action. If the teacher waits for the skill to be completed, the student may not pair the "no" with the incorrect part of the skill.

Tangible and generalized reinforcers should always be delivered in conjunction with social consequences. The reason for this rule is that we frequently use tangible or generalized reinforcers to exaggerate the feedback we wish to give a student. However, it will be necessary to eliminate those exaggerated consequences when the behavior has reached the desired level of performance. The social consequences, if not exaggerated, are considered natural and may be used to maintain the behavior after the exaggerated consequences are eliminated. The discussion on fading which follows describes the techniques more fully.

The final rule relative to consequences is that they should not be weak. As with "weak" cues, this term includes many faults. A verbal consequence should always be loud enough to be heard. A tangible consequence must be presented so that the student has sufficient opportunity to enjoy it. For instance, reinforcing a student with free play and removing it two minutes later will rarely be considered as reinforcement by the student; more likely he will perceive it as a tantalizer. Finally, if total communication is being used with a student, a verbal consequence must contain both the spoken words and the appropriate manual signs. The absence of either makes the consequence weak.

Shaping and Fading

Shaping is a process by which the student is reinforced for behaviors that are not quite at the criterion level the teacher may desire, but that begin to approximate that criterion level. In behavioral terms, this process is called the reinforcement of successive approximations of the terminal behavior. In the training of staff in these techniques, the term *shaping* is used. Let us illustrate. Learning to throw a ball overhand requires a certain motion and accuracy at a specified distance. In teaching the student this skill, the teacher's initial efforts are to develop a smooth overhand throwing motion. After that has been achieved, a prescribed degree of accuracy is achieved by having the student throw at a target. The percentage of accuracy is gradually increased at a short distance. When the prescribed criterion level of accuracy is reached, the distance is increased. For shaping to enhance the learning situation, the teacher must be very precise as to what standard of performance is acceptable from the student at a given time.

Within the *Data Based Gymnasium*, the individual task analyses which comprise the curriculum are organized as shaping procedures. Therefore, the entire teaching sequence for each behavior is already embodied in the task analysis for that behavior, pinpointing the intermediate behaviors necessary to be mastered prior to learning the terminal behavior. In cases where additional shaping is necessary beyond that contained in the curriculum, the teacher is responsible for preparing those additional sequences. This technique, called *branching*, is discussed in Chapter 6.

Fading is defined as the gradual elimination of reinforcers or cues. For instance, in the discussion under consequences, it was pointed out that, as soon as possible, the student should respond to the natural consequences of the environment. Therefore, every effort is made to gradually fade or eliminate the exaggerated reinforcers such as food, ringing bells, and tokens, leaving only the social reinforcer or natural consequence. Initially, the student may be rewarded with food and social praise every time she performs the behavior. After the behavior is established as part of the student's repertoire of behaviors, she may be given food only every other time the behavior is performed, although she receives social praise for each correct response. Later, the food is given every third time, then every fourth time, until finally the food is eliminated altogether, leaving only the social praise. The tangible reinforcer (food in this case) is then reserved for the teaching of new behaviors. Social praise given each time a student performs a behavior is not really a natural consequence, but rather exaggerated social praise. Thus, we also systematically fade this exaggerated social praise just as we do other tangible reinforcers. The end results are social reinforcers delivered intermittently.

Fading also refers to the fading of cues. This process, like the shaping process, is usually inherent within the curriculum sequence. For instance, when teaching a severely handicapped student to touch his toes, initially the teacher may model for the student, give the verbal cue "Touch your toes" and provide physical assistance to accomplish the task. During the teaching process, the cue of physical assistance is gradually eliminated, requiring the student to perform more of the task independently. After the physical assistance is completely faded from the program, the model will be faded, leaving only the verbal cue.

Summary

This chapter does not purport to be a comprehensive overview of behavioral principles. The chapter's purpose is to acquaint the reader with the learning principles utilized in the *Data Based Gymnasium*. Thus, we have chosen to discuss those items which the reader needs to be familiar with to understand the remainder of the book. A single chapter such as this is inadequate to discuss all the principles and ramifications of behavior modification and its accompanying teaching methodology. A complete introduction to the theory and its methodology written for parents and teachers is contained in the book *Isn't it Time He Outgrew This?* by Baldwin, Fredericks, and Brodsky (1972) and in pamphlets by Vance Hall (1971). More detailed discussions for those interested in expanding their knowledge about behavior modification are contained in Bijou and Baer (1966); Millenson (1967); Ullman and Krasner (1965); Ulrich, Stachnik, and Mabry (1966, 1970, 1974); Verhave (1966); and Krumboltz & Krumboltz (1973). This chapter provides only an overview which hopefully will allow the reader to understand the learning approach and methodology utilized in the *Data Based Gymnasium*.

Socialization and Inappropriate Behaviors | 3

Socialization includes many areas that cannot be put into convenient curricular slots such as language, motor activities, self-help, or cognition. Consequently, both the term and the curricular area become a catch-all for many aspects of curriculum. Yet there is occasional overlap or at least a strong interrelationship with other parts of the curriculum. For instance, students cannot engage in certain types of socialization, such as responding to others or to play activities, without the previous acquisition of either language activities and/or motor activities. Therefore, when a training program is initiated in the area of socialization, the skills which the student possesses in the other curricular areas must be considered.

As the discussion about socialization unfolds, the need for individualized programming for students will become quite obvious. Socialization skills cannot be prescribed in the same manner for all students. Of course, the teacher can require certain behaviors in her schoolroom that apply to all students, such as picking up toy areas when finished playing and responding when addressed; yet the degree of verbalization and the type of response may vary with each student. Most parents want their children to be "well behaved." However, when one examines the child in an individual home, the definitions of "well behaved" vary considerably. Some parents insist on the use of "please" and "thank you," while others never attend to such remarks. Thus, an individual program for each student in the area of socialization has to be prescribed. This prescription should be developed by both the parents and the teacher. For some students the program will be minimal. For other students, those who exhibit severe behavioral problems, the major emphasis of the entire instructional program initially will be the remediation of those inappropriate behaviors.

Types of Socialization

Prior to assessing a student's current functioning level and needs as related to social skills, it is important to know what types of skills socialization encompasses.

Social Interaction

Social interaction has been described as consisting of five basic components (Williams, Hamre-Nietupski, Pumpian, McDaniel-Marx, & Wheeler, 1978). First, the student must recognize the appropriate time and place for a social interaction, during free time rather than during instruction, for example. The next two components involve initiating an interaction or receiving requests for interaction. Initiating an interaction means asking another individual to engage in an activity, while receiving requests for interaction includes accepting or declining the initiation. These behaviors can be adapted to the student's functioning level in terms of communication. For example, a nonverbal student could initiate an interaction by pointing to a picture on a communication board or by using sign language. When invited to participate in an activity, he could use the same means to indicate "yes" or "no."

The fourth component of social interaction involves actual participation in the activity (sustaining an activity). For example, once the student has accepted a request from another student to play kickball, he should actually participate in the game. Finally, the individual must terminate the activity, which includes the ability to recognize that the activity is over and to perform any tasks involved in terminating it, such as putting equipment away.

Play Activities

Socialization also includes play activities. The "normal" child, as he grows, first engages in solitary play, then moves to parallel play with other children. In solitary play a child plays with toys or objects without attempting to interact with others. Parallel play can be defined as a child playing independently but close to another child, possibly imitating the other but generally not interacting or cooperating in any way (i.e., playing side-by-side in a sand box). The next step in the development of play activities is cooperative play—play where children use the same toys or engage in the same activities and exhibit some interaction. Examples of this type of play would be ball-related games, table games, or playing on a swing with one child pushing another. Parents frequently become disturbed because their child is slow in reaching the cooperative stage and go to counselors to determine how to teach their child to engage in cooperative play. It is not unthinkable that the same problem may arise with handicapped children. Moreover, handicapped children may be reluctant to engage in parallel play; in fact, many handicapped children are noted for perseverating behavior. They play with the same toy or the same object over and over in the same way day after day. Parents tend to become upset by this tendency and desire to extend the range of the child's interests. The teacher certainly should also be concerned if this type of perseveration persists.

Children learn through play and thus it is important that they engage in a variety of play activities. Consequently, those children who perseverate in one activity should be encouraged to engage in other activities and may need an individual program to ensure that this occurs. Such a program would, of course, put the child in a situation where he would have the opportunity to play with those objects.

Programming Socialization Behaviors

The objective of socialization programs should be to teach the student to engage in a variety of solitary and cooperative social activities at the appropriate time, place, and frequency. Selected activities and the social skills related to the task (initiating, receiving, sustaining, terminating) can be task analyzed and then taught using several different instructional procedures. Peer modeling, object proximity (physical placement of objects to elicit spontaneous responses), and increasing levels of assistance have been used successfully.

The principles of programming for inappropriate behaviors that will be described in the next section can also be applied to socialization programming. An example of a social skills program will be included in the examples which follow to illustrate that the same data forms and techniques are applicable.

Types of Inappropriate Behaviors

One of the major areas subsumed under socialization is the control of inappropriate behaviors or behavior problems. Inappropriate behaviors include those behaviors which appear to be abnormal because of the specific movement involved, the frequency of the response, or the situation in which the behavior occurs. Individuals who engage in excessive inappropriate behavior (i.e., body rocking, head banging, tantrumming) will not readily learn to interact socially until the behaviors are decreased. Therefore, programs to decrease undesirable behavior should focus not only on the remediation of the inappropriate behavior but also reinforce appropriate compatible behavior.

This chapter cannot discuss all the ramifications or techniques for remediation of inappropriate behaviors. What it does propose to do is to provide the general philosophy under which the data based gymnasium operates and to demonstrate the techniques for data keeping and data management of behavior programs in that environment.

Principles of Behavior Programming

A child who requires remediation of an inappropriate behavior usually has been engaging in the behavior to be remediated over a period of time. Moreover, adults who have tried to remediate these behaviors usually have tried various approaches for only short periods of time, none sufficiently long enough to allow any favorable behavior change. Not seeing an immediate change, they switch to a different strategy. Thus, there usually has been a history of inconsistency with the child. Therefore, one of the underlying principles on which all behavior programming must be based is the gaining of consistency in the actions of the adult or adults to the behaviors of the child. To ensure that consistency is achieved, a treatment should be maintained for a minimum of one week prior to consideration of change of that program. Typically, when a teacher or parent implements a new program, the child will test the program as it represents a new response by the adult. This results in an increase in the child's inappropriate behavior. Rather than changing the program at that point, it should be continued for at least one week to determine if the behavior is reduced after the initial increase.

The second major principle under which behavior programs in the data based gymnasium operate is that the end goal is to bring the child's behavior under the natural consequences of the environment. Considering this goal, most programming should start with the use of natural consequences, using social reinforcement, verbal corrections, and ignoring. The use of tangible reinforcers or token systems should only be initiated after it has been demonstrated that consistent social reinforcers will not achieve the desired behavior. Generally, the more complex a program, the more difficult it will be to implement with consistency.

Areas of Inappropriate Behaviors

In order to increase consistency of treatment, inappropriate behaviors have been categorized into four major areas: self-indulgence, noncompliance, aggression, and self-stimulation or self-destruction. Categorizing behaviors allows the teacher to apply a set of consequences (rules of thumb) to inappropriate behaviors. The teacher tries the rule of thumb remediation before placing the student in a formal behavior program. Frequently, the rule of thumb procedure will remediate the inappropriate behavior, thereby negating the necessity for a formal behavior program. Sometimes, a behavior will seem not to fall into a single category; for instance, the student who tantrums when told to do something. The teacher needs to recognize that the student is exhibiting two inappropriate behaviors—tantrumming and non-compliance, and these should be treated as two behaviors.

Self-indulgent Behavior. Self-indulgent behaviors include crying, pouting, sulking, screaming, tantrumming, repetitive activities designed to irritate, and nonsense noises not considered as self-stimulation. The rule of thumb for handling self-indulgent behaviors is to ignore the student until the behavior is discontinued for a short period of time, then socially reinforce appropriate behavior.

Noncompliant Behavior.   The second behavior area includes all forms of noncompliant behaviors: the student who says, "No" when asked to do something, the student who does not do something because he forgets, and the student who chooses not to do what is asked. It includes the nonperformance of routine behaviors. It also encompasses the student who does the required task but does it poorly, sloppily, or incompletely, and the student who does what he is asked but only after repeated commands or requests by his parents. Finally, this behavior area includes the student who does what he is asked but only with much argument and hassle.

Upon the occurrence of a noncompliant behavior, the rule of thumb is that the teacher should ignore noncompliant verbalizations, lead the student physically through the task, or refuse to let the student engage in an activity until he follows through with the original request. Socially reinforce the same student each time he complies to any commands given.

Aggressive Behavior. Aggression is a verbal or physically hostile act toward another person or object. Such behaviors as hitting, pinching, pushing, biting, and destroying property are included under this heading. Verbal aggression, such as cursing or screaming at someone, can also be included in this area, although it is often considered a self-indulgent behavior. The rule of thumb for remediating aggressive behavior is that it be punished immediately with a verbal reprimand and removal of the student from any activity. Social reinforcement should be given when the student is interacting appropriately with other persons or objects.

Self-stimulatory or Self-destructive Behavior.   This category includes repetitive behaviors that interfere with learning because the student blocks out other appropriate stimuli. Behaviors such as head banging, eye gouging, hand flapping, and ruminating would be included in this category. These behaviors can occur at a very high frequency in many environments, or at a very low frequency in one environment. A formal behavior program needs to be implemented for this type of behavior.

Steps for Behavior Programming

All behavior intervention programs and all programs to improve socialization have seven steps:

1. Pinpointing and accurately defining the behavior
2. Collecting baseline data
3. Establishing a terminal objective
4. Designing and implementing the behavior program
5. Analyzing the data
6. Modifying the program
7. Maintaining the behavior change over time, as well as across settings and persons

Each of these steps is discussed below.

Pinpointing and Accurately Defining the Behavior

First, it is necessary to define precisely the behavior targeted for possible treatment. Included in this definition is an observable description of the behavior, the environment(s) in which it occurs, and the category in which it would best fit. All dimensions of the behavior should be noted so that if one dimension changes, the teacher will be aware of it. For example, a tantrumming student may be throwing himself on the ground, screaming, and kicking. As this behavior is treated, data indicate no reduction in the number or length of the tantrums. However, when observing the student, the teacher notices that the student has ceased throwing himself on the ground and only stands and screams. The throwing himself on the ground and kicking, which was part of the original definition of the tantrum, have disappeared. Thus, it can be concluded that the treatment procedures used were effective in that they produced a less severe form of the behavior. The teacher faced with this change of intensity must proceed on the assumption that the behavior is improving. Normally, inappropriate behaviors are measured by frequency and/or duration. The intensity of the behavior adds another dimension of measurement.

Collecting Baseline Data

After the behavior has been precisely defined, baseline data should be obtained. Baseline data are a measurement of the parameters of the behavior prior to the introduction of a specific treatment. During the collection of baseline data, the behavior should be treated exactly as it was prior to initiating the baseline. Baseline data can be compared to subsequent treatment data to measure change in the behavior and thus to determine the treatment's effectiveness.

Ideally, baseline data should be collected for one week or with a minimum of three observations. If the behavior improves during baseline conditions, that treatment should be continued without initiating a new program.

There are several ways to measure behavior, depending upon how often the behavior occurs, and how much time and staff are available to observe the behavior. Figure 3.1 shows the form on which behavior is tallied, as well as an example of baseline data being recorded on four different behaviors: tantrumming, noncompliance, aggression, and appropriate play. Each behavior is measured with at least one of four methods: frequency, duration, percent, and interval recording.

Frequency. Frequency is simply a measurement of how often a behavior occurs during a specified time period. For instance, a teacher may count the number of times a student tantrums per day, as shown in Figure 3.1 Other behaviors that lend themselves to frequency counting include aggression, talk-outs, correct and incorrect responses, attendance, swearing, hand raising, and incidents of sharing. The advantage of using a frequency measure is that it can be used with a wide variety of classroom behaviors without disrupting the regular routine. However, if a behavior is occurring at a very high rate or lasts for an extended period of time, a frequency measure would generally be inappropriate. Other methods besides paper and pencil can be used for frequency recording, such as hand-held counters or marks on a chalkboard. The following formula can be used to calculate the frequency of occurrence of a behavior (each of these steps is discussed below):

BEHAVIOR TREATMENT DATA FORM

Name ___Bill___

Date Recording Initiated: ___1/19/85___   Date Recording Terminated: ___1/23/85___

BEHAVIORS	1/19/85	1/20/85	1/21/85	1/22/85	1/23/85	TOTAL	SUMMARY
Tantrumming – Number	I	II	I	III	II	9 1.8/day	
Length	5 min.	4 4	4	4 2 3	3 1	30 $\overline{X}$ = 3.3	
Complies	卌	II	卌 I	IIII	卌	22	
Does not comply	卌 III	卌 卌 III	卌 卌	卌 IIII	卌 I	46 % = 32%	
Hits peers	I	I		II	I	5 $\overline{X}$ = 1.0	
Appropriate play (Time sampling – 2 min. intervals for 20 min.)	卌 I	卌	卌 II	IIII	卌 II	29/100 29%	
Inappropriate play	卌 卌 IIII	卌 卌 卌	卌 卌 IIII	卌 卌 卌 I	卌 卌 III	72/100 72%	

Figure 3.1 Baseline data for Bill for tantrumming, aggression, noncompliance, and appropriate play.

$$\frac{\text{Total number of occurrences}}{\text{Total time behavior was observed}} = \frac{\text{Rate of occurrence per}}{\text{minute/hour/day}}$$

Example: $\frac{9 \text{ tantrums}}{5 \text{ days}}$ = 1.8 tantrums per day

Duration.   Duration measures are used to determine the length of time a behavior is performed by an individual, such as tantrumming, on-task behavior, or time spent in cooperative play. Duration is usually recorded with a stopwatch, accumulating the number of seconds or minutes the behavior is observed. This method of measurement yields a precise record of the length of occurrence of a behavior, but requires the continuous attention of the observer and would generally be inappropriate for high frequency behaviors of short duration. The following formula is used to calculate duration:

$$\frac{\text{Total length of all occurrences}}{\text{Total number of occurrences}} = \frac{\text{Average length of each}}{\text{occurrence}}$$

Example: $\frac{30 \text{ minutes}}{9 \text{ tantrums}}$ = an average of 3.3 min. per tantrum

Percent.   Percentage reporting is a measurement of how often a behavior occurs out of how often the behavior could possibly have occurred. This method is especially useful to measure compliance on following gymnasium rules. The formula is as follows:

$$\frac{\text{Number of compliances}}{\text{Total number of commands delivered}} = \text{\% of compliance}$$

Example: $\frac{22 \text{ compliances}}{68 \text{ commands delivered}}$ = 32% compliance

Interval Recording.   The inverval recording method involves dividing an observation session into equal periods of time and recording the occurrence or nonoccurrence of a behavior during these intervals. Interval recording can be of two types: continuous and time sampling. During continuous interval recording, the teacher's attention must be directed toward the behavior during the entire observation period, noting for each interval of the time period whether or not the behavior occurred. The observer must also have a method of timing each interval, such as a kitchen timer, stopwatch, or portable tape recorder with prerecorded interval counts.

Time sampling, however, does not require the observer's continuous attention, because a data point is recorded only at the end of each interval. For example, attending behavior can be measured during a 20-minute period that is divided into 10 two-minute intervals. At the end of each two-minute interval, the observer looks at the student and records whether he was attending at that instant (see example below). This procedure results in a percentage of intervals that the student was attending in relation to the total number of intervals observed.

20-minute time sample

Minute	2	4	6	8	10	12	14	16	18	20
Behavior	+	O	+	+	O	O	O	O	+	+

In the example above, the individual was attending five out of ten intervals, or 50% of the time the observer sampled his behavior. The general formula for interval recording follows:

$$\frac{\text{Number of times behavior occurred}}{\text{Number of intervals observed in behavior}} = \text{\% of intervals student engaged in behavior}$$

Recommended Measurement Methods for Categories of Behavior

1. Self-indulgent behavior—measure the frequency and duration of the behavior.
2. Noncompliant behavior—measure the number of incidences of compliance and noncompliance to obtain a percentage of compliance.
3. Aggressive behavior—measure frequency and/or duration of the behavior.
4. Self-stimulatory behavior—if the frequency of the behavior is low, measure frequency and duration. If the onset of the behavior is difficult to observe and the frequency is high, interval recording may be more reliable. If the behavior occurs across a number of environments, baseline data should be collected for each environment. Treatment may not generalize across environments and it may be necessary to design treatments for several environments.

Summarizing the Baseline Data. Baseline data are computed after completion of the baseline period, referring to the formulas given previously. The date of observation and the summary of data should be recorded on the Behavior Program Cover Sheet shown in Figure 3.2 and Figure 3.3. The collection procedures should also be specified, including the method of measurement used, the amount of time per day observed, and the location of the observation. Treatment of the behavior during the baseline period should also be recorded.

Establishing a Terminal Objective

After the baseline data have been computed and the data substantiate the existence of a problem, a terminal objective should be established for each program to be initiated, using baseline data to determine a reasonable objective. Parents should be consulted and should approve not only the objective but also the proposed treatment program. It should be included as part of the IEP.

The program objective should be stated in positive terms if possible and should include the environment in which the behavior is to be treated, the criterion for acceptable performance, and the duration for which the criterion of acceptable performance must be maintained. This objective is entered on the form shown in Figure 3.2 and Figure 3.3. In the case of Bill, two programs were felt to be serious enough to warrant treatment, command compliance and appropriate play with others. The objective chosen for command compliance was to "increase command compliance in the gym to 80 percent for three consecutive weeks" (Figure 3.2). The objective specified for appropriate play with others was "to increase appropriate play with others during free time to 80 percent during a 10-minute sample for three consecutive weeks." When setting up objectives for compliance, and self-indulgent and self-stimulatory behaviors, never seek perfection. An 80 percent compliance rate has been found to be achievable by most students. Self-indulgent behaviors can usually be lowered to one or two occurrences per week of a duration of two minutes or less.

Designing and Implementing the Behavior Program

As indicated previously, most programs initially conducted in the gymnasium will use natural social consequences for behaviors in order to establish a consistent system of responding to the student. In many cases, this may be sufficient to bring the behavior under control. This approach is easy to conduct and introduces no artificial consequences which the teacher or parent may have difficulty ac-

BEHAVIOR PROGRAM COVER SHEET

Name _Bill_ **Date Initiated** _1/26/85_ **Date Terminated** _____

Program to be Conducted: ☐ Home   ☒ School   ☐ Both

BASELINE DATA

Collection Procedure: Record all commands and all compliances all day (9:00-2:00)

Date	Data	Comments and Treatment
1/19-1/23	22/68 = 32%	Socially correct all noncompliance.

PROGRAM OBJECTIVE: To increase command compliance in the gym to 80% for 3 consecutive weeks.

SYNOPSIS OF PROGRAM

Date	Weekly Total	Treatment No.	Date	Weekly Total	Treatment No.

POST TREATMENT FOLLOW-UP

Date	Weekly Total	Treatment No.	Date	Weekly Total	Treatment No.

If program terminated, state reason: _____

Figure 3.2. Program cover sheet for compliance program for Bill.

BEHAVIOR PROGRAM COVER SHEET

Name __Bill__   **Date Initiated** __1/26/85__   **Date Terminated** _____

Program to be Conducted: ☐ Home   ☒ School   ☐ Both

BASELINE DATA

Collection Procedure: Record occurrence of appropriate play with others at end of each 30-second interval of a 10-minute sample.

Date	Data	Comments and Treatment
1/19-1/23	29/100 = 29%	Socially correct inappropriate play with others.

PROGRAM OBJECTIVE: To increase appropriate play with others during free time to 80% during a 10-minute time sample for 3 consecutive weeks.

SYNOPSIS OF PROGRAM

Date	Weekly Total	Treatment No.	Date	Weekly Total	Treatment No.

POST TREATMENT FOLLOW-UP

Date	Weekly Total	Treatment No.	Date	Weekly Total	Treatment No.

If program terminated, state reason: _____

Figure 3.3. Program cover sheet for appropriate play program for Bill.

cepting or implementing. Moreover, if the program is successful using social consequences, there will be no need to fade out the artificial consequences.

The form used in the gymnasium for the designing of a program is shown in Figures 3.4 and 3.5. Figure 3.4 shows the treatment for remediation of noncompliance. Each treatment is numbered and consequences prescribed for the occurrence of the desirable and undesirable behavior. In Figure 3.4, the student is to be socially reinforced for compliance. For noncompliance he is to be told, "No," recued, led through the behavior, and then socially reinforced. This latter treatment is the basic correction procedure used in the gymnasium for young students or students who are severely disabled. Figure 3.5 shows the behavior program treatment form for programming appropriate play with others. When appropriate play is observed, the behavior is to be socially reinforced. When inappropriate play is observed, the student is socially corrected and reminded to play appropriately.

BEHAVIOR PROGRAM TREATMENT FORM

Name ____Bill____

BEHAVIOR TO INCREASE

BEHAVIOR TO DECREASE
Noncompliance to spontaneous commands

Treatment Number	Date	When BEHAVIOR TO INCREASE occurs, do this:	When BEHAVIOR TO DECREASE occurs, do this:
1		Socially reinforce.	Socially correct by saying "No." Repeat cue, physically assist, and give mild social reinforcement.
2		Socially reinforce and pair with point on chart. Five points earn 10 minutes of free time.	Same as above.

Figure 3.4. Behavior program treatment form for Bill's compliance program.

BEHAVIOR PROGRAM TREATMENT FORM

Name ___Bill_____

BEHAVIOR TO INCREASE   **BEHAVIOR TO DECREASE**

Inappropriate play with others

Treatment Number	Date	When BEHAVIOR TO INCREASE occurs, do this:	When BEHAVIOR TO DECREASE occurs, do this:
1		Socially reinforce at approximately three-minute intervals of appropriate play.	Socially correct each interval of inappropriate play and remind student to play appropriately. When he resumes appropriate play, give mild social reinforcement.

Figure 3.5.   Behavior program treatment form for Bill's appropriate play program.

Treatment schematics have been developed as general guidelines to aid in the designing of a treatment program, but not every behavior program will automatically fit into these schematics. The schematics that follow are divided into two columns, one indicating the consequence for the desirable behavior (behavior to be increased) and a second indicating the consequence for the behavior to be lessened. This procedure ensures that the student is always provided with an alternative desirable response rather than merely encouraged to eliminate an undesirable behavior.

The schematics should be read horizontally so that each treatment includes two consequences: one for the desirable behavior and one for the undesirable behavior. The teacher has to choose alternatives in the columns on several of the schematics: is the treatment for a younger student or individual with severe handicaps, or for an older individual? (Figure 3.6).

For the younger (preschool age) or severely handicapped student, reinforcement usually needs to be immediate to ensure acquisition

TREATMENT FOR SELF-INDULGENT BEHAVIOR

When BEHAVIOR TO BE IMPROVED occurs, do this:		When BEHAVIOR TO BE LESSENED occurs, do this:	
1. Socially Reinforce		1. Ignore	
2. Socially Reinforce		2. *When adult cannot ignore,* Time out	*When adult can ignore,* Ignore
3. *Younger or severely handicapped* Social Reinforcement	*Older* Tokens	3. *When adult cannot ignore,* Time out	*When adult can ignore,* Ignore
3a. Social Reinforcement + Tangible Reinforcer "A"	Tokens + Tangible Reinforcer "A"	3a. Time out	Ignore
3b. Social Reinforcement + Tangible Reinforcer "B"	Tokens + Tangible Reinforcer "B"	3b. Time out	Ignore
3c. Social Reinforcement + Tangible Reinforcer "C"	Tokens + Tangible Reinforcer "C"	3c. Time out	Ignore
4. Tangible Reinforcer + Bonus	Bonus System	4. Time out	Ignore
5. Tangible Reinforcer + Bonus	Bonus System	5. Time out	Time out
6. Tangible Reinforcer + Bonus	Bonus System	6. Punisher	Punisher

Figure 3.6. Treatment schematic for self-indulgent behavior.

of a behavior. However, a student with severe handicaps can learn to function within a more complicated reinforcement system, such as a token economy. Token systems have been effective with this population when specific procedures have been implemented to assist the student in associating between the token and its back-up reinforcer. Basically, the procedures consist of requesting a behavior, reinforcing it immediately upon occurrence with a token and praise, and immediately exchanging the token for a back-up reinforcer. This cycle is repeated until the student shows evidence of making the association between the token and back-up reinforcer. Once this occurs, the exchange schedule can be increased so that the student must accumulate more than one token before an exchange is made.

The schematic in Figure 3.6 and the figures following refers to different types of reinforcers. "Tangible Reinforcer A" refers to the first tangible reinforcer used. "Reinforcer B" implies that "Reinforcer A" was unsuccessful, so a new item is being introduced. The schematic only shows tangible reinforcers A, B, and C, though this is not meant to be limiting. Tangible reinforcers or combinations of them continue to be used until all available have been tried before increasing the power of the punisher (lines 5 and 6). During treatment #4 (Figure 3.6), a bonus is introduced. A bonus is a reinforcer given for good behavior maintaining over time, such as ½ hour, 2 hours, ½ day, or a number of days without a tantrum.

The teacher may also have to make a decision as to whether the behavior can be ignored. Ignoring a behavior assumes that previous attention to the behavior was reinforcing, and after removing that reinforcement the behavior should decrease. In a gymnasium, it may be difficult to control peer reinforcement, in which case the teacher may want to consider time out as an alternative strategy (see the right hand column of Figure 3.6). It is also prescribed that mild aggressions be ignored (see Figure 3.7). If the student's behavior is destructive to property or can hurt others, the behavior should not be ignored. Even for minor aggressions like taps or shoves, the teacher must determine her tolerance for the presence of the behavior, taking into consideration the safety of others and the disruptive effect in the gymnasium.

It is important to note that only one component of the behavior program changes with each successive treatment, and that the magnitude of the reinforcer is always increased prior to the introduction of a punisher. For example, following the schematic for non-compliant behavior (see Figure 3.8), the first treatment involves socially reinforcing compliance and socially correcting noncompliance. A social correction consists of giving the student verbal and/or nonverbal negative feedback as soon as the undesirable behavior occurs, restating the cue and firmly physically assisting the student to perform the appropriate behavior. If this treatment is not successful, the second treatment is considered – adding a tangible reinforcer to the consequences for compliance. Noncompliance continues to be socially corrected. The reinforcer is continually increased up to treatment #4, at which point time out is implemented in place of a social correction. The schematic for self-stimulatory/self-destructive behavior is shown in Figure 3.9.

TREATMENT FOR AGGRESSIVE BEHAVIORS

When BEHAVIOR TO BE IMPROVED occurs, do this:		When BEHAVIOR TO BE LESS-ENED occurs, do this:	
1. Socially reinforce		1. *If behavior is mild,* Ignore	*If behavior is not mild,* Time out
2. *Younger or severely handicapped* Social Reinforcer + Tangible Reinforcer "A"	*Older* Tokens + Tangible Reinforcer "A"	2. Ignore	Time out
2a. Social Reinforcer + Tangible Reinforcer "B"	Tokens + Tangible Reinforcer "B"	2a. Ignore	Time out
2b. Social Reinforcer + Tangible Reinforcer "C"	Tokens + Tangible Reinforcer "C"	2b. Ignore	Time out
2c. Social Reinforcer + Tangible Reinforcer "D" + Bonus	Tokens + Bonus	2c. Ignore	Time out
3. Tangible Reinforcer + Bonus	Tokens + Bonus	3. Time out	Punish
4. Tangible Reinforcer + Bonus	Tokens + Bonus	4. Punish	Punish

Figure 3.7. Treatment schematic for aggressive behavior.

TREATMENT FOR NONCOMPLIANT BEHAVIOR

When BEHAVIOR TO BE IMPROVED occurs, do this:		When BEHAVIOR TO BE LESS-ENED occurs, do this:
1. Socially reinforce		1. Socially correct
2. *Younger or severely handicapped* Social Reinforcer + Tangible Reinforcer "A"	*Older* Tokens + Tangible Reinforcer "A"	2. Socially correct
2a. Social Reinforcement + Tangible Reinforcer "B"	Tokens + Tangible Reinforcer "B"	2a. Socially correct
2b. Social Reinforcement + Tangible Reinforcer "C"	Tokens + Tangible Reinforcer "C"	2b. Socially correct
2c. Social Reinforcement + Tangible Reinforcer "D"	Tokens + Tangible Reinforcer "D"	2c. Socially correct
3. Tangible Reinforcer + Bonus	Tokens + Bonus	3. Socially correct
4. Tangible Reinforcer + Bonus	Tokens + Bonus	4. Time out
5. Tangible Reinforcer + Bonus	Tokens + Bonus	5. Punisher

Figure 3.8. Treatment schematic for noncompliant behavior.

TREATMENT FOR SELF-STIMULATORY BEHAVIOR

When BEHAVIOR TO BE IMPROVED occurs, do this:		When BEHAVIOR TO BE LESSENED occurs, do this:
1. Socially reinforce		1. Socially correct (plus restraint)
2. *Younger or severely handicapped* Social Reinforcer + Tangible Reinforcer "A"	*Older* Tokens + Tangible Reinforcer "A"	2. Socially correct (plus restraint)
2a. Social Reinforcer + Tangible Reinforcer "B"	Tokens + Tangible Reinforcer "B"	2a. Socially correct (plus restraint)
2b. Social Reinforcer + Tangible Reinforcer "C"	Tokens + Tangible Reinforcer "C"	2b. Socially correct (plus restraint)
2c. Social Reinforcer + Tangible Reinforcer "D"	Tokens + Tangible Reinforcer "D"	2c. Socially correct (plus restraint)
3. Tangible Reinforcer + Bonus	Tokens + Bonus	3. Socially correct (plus restraint)
4. Tangible Reinforcer + Bonus	Tokens + Bonus	4. Time out
5. Tangible Reinforcer + Bonus	Tokens + Bonus	5. Punisher

Figure 3.9. Treatment schematic for self-stimulatory/self-destructive behavior.

There are guidelines for determining a reinforcement schedule for each of the categories of behaviors. Noncompliant behaviors should initially be reinforced for each compliance. After the behavior reaches the criterion level of the terminal objective, the reinforcement schedule should be modified by eliminating through a fading process all tangible reinforcers. Rules of politeness would dictate that social reinforcers are to be delivered on a continuous reinforcement schedule. In other words, if a student is asked to do something and complies, the very minimum reinforcer should be "Thank you."

The determination of the reinforcement schedule for nonaggression, non-self-indulgent, and non-self-stimulatory behavior often proves more troublesome. To determine an appropriate schedule, divide the total amount of time observed by the number of occurrences. For example, if an individual displayed nine aggressions in six hours, convert the hours to minutes (6 hours x 60 minutes = 360 minutes) and divide by nine. This gives an average of 1 aggression every 40 minutes. Reinforcement should be delivered at a rate of one-half the average time between occurrences. In this example, reinforcement should be delivered once every 20 minutes that the individual is not aggressive. If that treatment is not successful, the teacher could reinforce at a higher frequency. After the individual meets success at the interval established; the length of time between reinforcers is gradually increased.

Analyzing the Data

Data are gathered daily on the form shown in Figure 3.1. These data are analyzed weekly and compared with the data of the previous week. They are recorded on the behavior program cover sheet shown in Figure 3.10. If the data show an improvement over the previous week, the program remains unchanged. For instance, Figure 3.10 shows the summary data for five weeks for Bill's compliance program. The data computed on Figure 3.10 shows a 32 percent compliance rate for baseline. During the first week of the program, that dated 1-30, the compliance rate increased to 39 percent. Notice on Figure 3.10 that under "Synopsis of Program," the number of the program entered is that which appears on the Behavior Program Treatment Form (Figure 3.4).

During the next week of the program, February 6, the compliance rate was 38 percent. This shows only a slight decrease from the previous week's 39 percent. Therefore, the teacher is now required to change the program. That change is entered on the Behavior Program Treatment Form. The program decided upon is labeled Program #2. Under "Behavior to be Improved," the teacher enters "Socially reinforce and pair with point on chart." Five points earn 10 minutes of free time (Figure 3.4). For noncompliance, the consequence has not changed. As shown in Figure 3.10, the data from Program #2 increase to 52 percent on February 13, then to 71 percent on February 20, and finally to 74 percent on February 27. As long as the program shows continual gain as the behavior approaches the criterion level, the program should not be changed.

There are some exceptions to the general rule that the program should be changed if there is no improvement over the previous week's data. An analysis of the current week's data may show a trend

BEHAVIOR PROGRAM COVER SHEET

Name __Bill__   **Date Initiated** __1/26/85__   **Date Terminated** _____

Program to be Conducted: □ Home   ☒ School   □ Both

BASELINE DATA

Collection Procedure: __Record all commands and all compliances all day__
__(9:00-2:00)__

Date	Data	Comments and Treatment
1/19-1/23	22/68 = 32%	Socially correct all noncompliance.

PROGRAM OBJECTIVE: To increase command compliance in the gym to 80% for 3 consecutive weeks.

SYNOPSIS OF PROGRAM

Date	Weekly Total	Treatment No.	Date	Weekly Total	Treatment No.
1/30	39%	1			
2/6	38%	1			
2/13	52%	2			
2/20	71%	2			
2/27	74%	2			

POST TREATMENT FOLLOW-UP

Date	Weekly Total	Treatment No.	Date	Weekly Total	Treatment No.

If program terminated, state reason: _____

Figure 3.10. Program cover sheet for compliance program for Bill after six weeks.

of improvement through the course of the week. This will most often occur when a new program has been established and the student, in testing the new program, shows an immediate increase in the inappropriate behavior. As the student realizes that the program is going to be administered in a consistent fashion, he begins to demonstrate a decrease in that behavior. The behavior most often cited in the literature for which this phenomenon occurs is a behavior such as tantrumming which, when initially ignored, usually increases in length and frequency before it begins to decrease. However, the experience of the Teaching Research Parent Clinic indicates that this phenomenon also occurs in other behaviors such as noncompliance and aggression. Therefore, the trend within the week needs to be examined to determine whether or not a reduction is occurring after this spontaneous increase.

Another exception to the rule involves unusual circumstances in the classroom. For instance, while the teacher is sick and a substitute teacher is employed, the program may not be conducted as consistently as prescribed. Consequently, the data would reflect this inconsistent response to the student's behavior. If the student has been absent for periods of time, it is better to gather at least three consecutive days of data before changing the program. In those behaviors in which two dimensions are measured, such as duration and frequency (see Figure 3.1, tantrumming), a change may only be manifested in one of those dimensions at a time. If such a change is manifested and improvement is shown, then the program should not be changed.

Modifying the Program

The entire process of analyzing data is based upon comparing the current week's data with that of the previous week. A dichotomous decision is made. If the data do not show improvement and do not fall into one of the exceptions previously described, then the program should be changed.

When the program is to be changed, the general rule is to increase the power of the reinforcers, leaving the punisher constant, until all reinforcers have been completely explored. Generally, reinforcers will be sufficient to modify the behavior without ever having to impose a punisher more severe than social correction. However, when positive approaches fail to reduce the problem behavior, it may become necessary to implement a more severe punishment procedure. The procedure selected should be based on the individual characteristics of the student and the behavior, the staff's ability to carry out the program in a consistent manner, the probability of successfully eliminating the behavior by implementing the procedure, and the ethical and legal aspects of the procedure (Gaylord-Ross, 1980).

Time out (from positive reinforcement) is employed as a treatment strategy at various stages in all four schematics. Time out, when applied contingently for the occurrence of an undesirable behavior, should eliminate the opportunity for the student to engage in any social interaction or receive any positive reinforcement. If time out does not result in a decrease in the undesirable behavior, it cannot be considered as a punisher for that student, and alternative treatments must be considered.

Time out can range from an informal to a formal treatment. An informal time out would consist of merely turning away from the student who is misbehaving. A more complex form of time out would involve sending the individual to a neutral location, such as a small, empty room with adequate lighting and ventilation.

The length of time out can also vary, depending on the individual's functioning level and behavior while in a time-out situation. Short time outs (one minute) can be jsut as effective as a time out that is 20 or 30 minutes long. If the student engages in inappropriate behavior when the time-out period has ended, the teacher should wait until the first quiet moment to remove the student from time out.

When a punisher is applied, it should be delivered immediately after the occurrence of the undesirable behavior. If the punishment is delayed for some reason, it may be best to wait for the next occurrence of the behavior rather than risk punishing the wrong behavior. Initial administration of the punishment should be at full intensity rather than successively increasing intensity with each occurrence of the behavior, which allows the individual to adapt to each successive degree of punishment.

As a general rule, the aversive consequence should be paired with a verbal reprimand (e.g., "No!" or "That's wrong!") so that through repeated pairings, the reprimand may become a conditioned stimulus to suppress the inappropriate behavior.

The teacher should be aware that, besides reducing the inappropriate behavior, less desirable side effects can occur when implementing a punisher. These can include a reduction in unpunished behaviors that may not be undesirable and/or emotional reactions such as anxiety or avoidance, or may cause the student to rebel. Because of these potential side effects, it is important for teachers to be extremely careful in their selection of a punisher.

Maintaining Behavior Change

After the objective for a program is achieved for the period of time specified in the program cover sheet (Figures 3.2 and 3.3) and all artificial reinforcers have been faded, the program is put on a maintenance schedule. The student should be responding to the natural consequences of the environment before the program is considered complete and placed on maintenance. For maintenance, the program is checked at one-month, three-month, and six-month intervals. This probing is done by retaking baseline data for one week at each time interval. If the data indicate that the behavior has not deteriorated, then no further action is necessary. If the data indicate that deterioration of the behavior has occurred to a degree unacceptable to either the parents or the teacher, the behavior program should be reinstated.

Gymnasium Management 4

Many readers may be familiar with the term *classroom management*, but few, if any, have used or observed in print the term *gymnasium management*. Essentially, the expressions are synonymous. The phrase gymnasium management highlights the fact that learning is learning regardless of the educational setting and that the gymnasium, like the classroom, must be managed to ensure educational gains. Gymnasium management, like classroom management, means the teacher must use everything at her disposal to accomplish instructional objectives. These include people, setting, curriculum and the administrative technique to bring them together.

The Physical Education Teacher

The person responsible for teaching physical education to the severely handicapped varies from school district to school district and from state to state. The options usually include one or two persons, the special educator or the physical educator. According to the Rules and Regulations for P.L. 94-142, it could be argued that technically either person is qualified. If the local school district has physical educators available to instruct nonhandicapped students, it seems logical that physical educators should be available to instruct handicapped students. In the eventuality that a physical educator is available to teach physical education to the severely handicapped, it is essential that this person work closely with the special education teacher. In short, it is necessary for the physical educator to understand not only the student's movement needs, but also basic information such as the student's reinforcement schedule and language capabilities.

The teacher of physical education for the severely handicapped must assume a role as manager of the learning environment. Students with major disabilities require educational settings in which they are instructed individually or in small groups. Such an arrangement is possible only if the teacher has assistants.

Volunteers

Successful implementation of the Oregon State University Teaching Research Model, whether in the classroom or the gymnasium, requires the availability of volunteers. They are frequently most responsible for conducting the individual motor skill acquisition program. Selecting and training volunteers is therefore a critical process. Even in those districts where physical educators teach the severely handicapped, the special educator normally assumes the lead role in the training of volunteers. The special process for the training of volunteers is found in Chapter 7.

Aides

Self-contained classrooms for the severely handicapped normally are staffed with a special educator and a professional aide. The latter individual assumes a variety of important functions – as a trainer and supervisor of the volunteers and, in the absence of the teacher, as the teacher's replacement.

The aide can also play an important part in the conduct of the physical education program. In districts without professionally trained physical educators, the aide's physical education responsibility is determined by the special education teacher in a manner similar to that for other program areas. The aide's role in such districts is primarily to assist in the transition of students from one teacher to another. Besides providing an important link between the classroom and gymnasium setting and assisting in the physical education instructional process, the aide can also help provide consistency in implementing language and behavior programs. Physical education teachers, although knowledgeable in the subject matter, often find themselves at a disadvantage in conducting programs for the severely handicapped because of their unique behaviors. Uncertainty about individual behaviors coupled with lack of information about or experience with individual students can be corrected by the presence of an aide who spends most of the day with the students.

The Gymnasium

The availability of a gymnasium is not essential for conducting appropriate physical education programs. For some students, the large open space of a gymnasium may actually inhibit learning. Many of the programs in the physical education curriculum can be conducted in a classroom, hallway, or some other available space. Regardless of the area used, the most important concept is to develop individualized programs without interruption. For some of the basic game skills like throwing and kicking, a larger area such as a cafeteria, hallway, or gymnasium is desirable so as not to disturb or endanger others. Equipment needed to conduct the physical education programs should include the following:

Mats (4'×6')	Basketballs
Sets of shapes:	Baseballs, bats, gloves
Circle (3' radius)	Softballs
Square (4' radius)	Volleyball
Triangle (4' equivalent sides)	Soccer ball
Rectangle (4'×2' sides)	Tricycle
Balls (4")	Bicycle
Balls (8½")	Hula hoops
Measuring tapes	Tennis balls
Classroom chairs	

Objectives

The major element in gymnasium management is the designation of long and short range instructional objectives for each student. These should be extracted from a curriculum with a detailed scope and equence of behavioral objectives. A description and some instructional sequences from such a curriculum are contained in Appendix A.

Curriculum, Assessment, and Data Keeping

Using the curriculum properly requires an initial assessment of the student, including a determination of the skills in the curriculum which he possesses and those which he does not possess. This initial assessment is necessary if the teacher is going to conduct individual programming of students to the extent specified in this model. In addition, the teacher needs an easy system of keeping track of the student's acquired skills as he moves through the instructional scope and sequence. Thus, a data keeping system that allows for initial assessment and easy updating of the student's program is mandatory in a good gymnasium management system. Chapter 6 discusses that system in detail.

The Pupils

The teacher needs to know the physical limitations that may alter the teaching approach to the student. Sensory deprivation, such as partial or total loss of sight or hearing, and all physical anomalies that may interfere with the student's movement capability must be determined. Understanding of the moderately and severely handicapped student also means knowing those activities and equipment that can serve as reinforcers for the student. Thus, a reinforcer list for each student is prepared and becomes an essential element in the gymnasium management system.

The Parents

A final component to complete the picture is the participation of parents, an essential part of the instruction team. Much instruction can be carried out by parents in the home. They not only can maintain skills their children have learned in physical education but also can actually accelerate learning. Thus coordination with parents is a vital element in gymnasium management. Chapter 10 gives the particulars of this coordination.

The Clipboard

Ongoing communication among the various individuals conducting programs for the handicapped is very important. Keeping the communication lines open helps maintain consistency in instruction and assists handicapped students in achieving their potential. A clipboard designed for each student assists in maintaining consistency. This management device evolved out of the need to build a communication system between volunteers, aides, and the teacher. It acts as the communication channel through which most instructional information is shared with the volunteers and aides. By reviewing the clipboard, the volunteer knows what programs need to be run and how they are to be conducted. Feedback or comments from the volunteer regarding the students' daily performance assists the teacher in making appropriate modifications. The clipboard management system frees the teacher to supervise volunteers, train new individuals, and monitor student progress.

Each student's clipboard contains a Weekly Cover Sheet (Figure 4.1) listing all the current physical education programs for that student. The volunteer, aide, or teacher initials the box that corresponds

to the day of the week a particular program was run. A circle in-
serted on any specific day means the skill is a priority item to be
taught that day. The volunteer may select any program if none of the
boxes have circles in them. Most students are limited to five programs. If the programs listed are run no more than 80 percent of the
time, a reduction should be made. For example, if there are five programs and the student has physical education daily, or five times per
week, the maximum number of programs possible would be 25. If
the student has less than 20 sessions of physical education, one of
the programs should be dropped. The number of programs is often
increased or decreased based upon the number of volunteers available to teach and the amount of available instructional time.

Weekly Cover Sheet

A sample Weekly Cover Sheet is shown in Figure 4.1. Jim, the
student for whom the cover sheet has been prepared, is scheduled
for four motor skill programs: (a) Basic Game Skills – Underhand
Strike; (b) Basic Game Skills – Underhand Throw; (c) Movement Concepts, Personal Space – Stand Heel to Toe; and (d) Leisure Skills – Go
Down A Slide. The initials on the right side of the form indicate
whether the program has been run and by whom. Blank squares
indicate that the program was not conducted. For instance, the chart
represents the situation as of Thursday immediately prior to the start
of class. "Basic Game Skills – Underhand Throw" was not conducted
on Wednesday. The circle opposite that program on Thursday indicates that it is a priority program and should be conducted first. The
cover sheet allows the teacher to determine programming priorities
at a glance. The Weekly Cover Sheet is often laminated with plastic
so that the form can be used over and over. The lamination also
protects the clipboard from moisture when outdoors.

Language and Consequence File Sheet

Immediately following the Weekly Cover Sheet is the Language
and Consequence File Sheet (Figure 4.2). This sheet lists the reinforcement file, skills to be generalized, receptive language level, expressive language level, as well as general comments.

The reinforcers are divided into two categories – primary/tangible
and social. Primary and tangible reinforcers include items such as
food, water juice, or any edible item the individual likes to consume.
As a general rule it is unnecessary to use reinforcers of this magnitude in the physical education setting. Much greater reliance is placed
on functional reinforcers which may be used if the student works hard

WEEKLY COVER SHEET

Name: Jim

Program	M	T	W	TH	F
1. Underhand Strike	JM	JM	JM		
2. Underhand Throw	JM	JM		○	
3. Stand Heel to Toe		(JM)	JM		
4. Go Down a Slide	JM	JM	JM		

Please Note: _____

_____

_____

_____

JM Signature of volunteer
O Denotes program priority

Figure 4.1 Sample weekly cover sheet.

for a designated time or number of trials. For example, permitting a youngster to engage in an enjoyable activity such as swinging on a rope for three minutes may be used as a functional reinforcer for working on a specific skill for fifteen minutes. The reinforcer selected should relate to the task being taught, and the student should find it enjoyable. Social reinforcers are used frequently with severely handicapped students. A social reinforcer may be a statement (e.g., "Good Job!") or something as simple as smiling at a student or patting him on the head. Social reinforcers are very important and should be used extensively with severely handicapped students.

In addition to the reinforcers used with the student, skills to be generalized are listed. The true test of learning and retention is whether the student can take the skill learned in a one-to-one instructional environment and use it in a related activity. For example,

LANGUAGE AND CONSEQUENCE FILE SHEET

Name: ___Jim_____

Reinforcement File	**SKILLS TO BE GENERALIZED:** (Give the child a chance to show you these new skills.)
PRIMARY/TANGIBLE:	
Swinging on a rope.	Climbing stairs.
Shooting baskets.	
Hitting the racquetball.	
Swinging on the bars.	
SOCIAL: (Examples)	
"Give me five!"	
"Super job!"	
"Nice going!"	
"Right on!"	

Receptive Language

1. Jim responds to two concept commands and is expected to follow through.
2. Be sure Jim is attending prior to giving a cue.

Expressive Language

1. Jim will emit one and two word responses.
2. Make Jim respond verbally to questions.
3. If Jim wants something have him ask for it.
4. Jim will imitate words if given the initial sound of the word.

General Comments

1. Jim must keep his hands to himself prior to starting a new trial.
2. Jim is right-handed.
3. Run the behavior treatment program if Jim strikes someone.

Figure 4.2. Sample language and consequence file sheet.

can a student who has learned to swim in a pool environment swim in other bodies of water such as a lake or pond?

The Receptive Language section defines to what degree the student understands spoken language. In Figure 4.2, the receptive language entry shows that Jim understands simple one- and two-concept word responses. The Expressive Language section describes the degree of language complexity that the student is able to emit. For instance, Figure 4.2, under expressive language, indicates that Jim emits one- and two-word responses and will imitate words when given the initial sound of the word.

The last section in Figure 4.2 is devoted to general comments, which include instructions on how to handle behavioral problems that may occur during the instructional period. Reference may also be made to other important instructional items such as hand and foot preference. For instance, Jim prefers to use his right hand when performing manipulative skills.

The main purpose of the Language and Consequence File Sheet is to ensure that those conducting one-to-one instruction use full strenght reinforcers with each individual, incorporate the appropriate cues to maximize the student's capability to respond to cues, and appropriately consequate behaviors unique to the student.

Placement Form

The Placement Form (Figure 4.3) follows the Language and Consequence File Sheet. (The placement process and form will be discussed in more depth in Chapter 5.) The Placement Form is a listing of all the skills task analyzed in the *Game, Exercise, and Leisure Sport Curriculum*. Its main purpose is to summarize the child's entry level skill and to identify the phase at which each skill is presently being performed.

Motor Skill Sequence Sheet

The Motor Skill Sequence Sheet, Figure 4.4, is a task-analyzed sequence of the skill into phases and steps. Since each phase builds on the preceding one, the volunteer can follow the program with minimal difficulty. This process also guarantees that students will be successful in mastering the skill.

Program Cover Sheet

The Program Cover Sheet, Figure 4.5, is a half-sheet covering the top half of the Data Sheet, Figure 4.6. Its purpose is to identify in

GAME, EXERCISE, AND LEISURE SPORT PLACEMENT FORM

For all skills listed below, cue by saying, "Watch me," demonstrate, and then use verbal and/or signed cue listed below.

SKILL	CUE	DATE	Placement Yes/No	DATE	Baseline #/Total	DATE	Posttest #/Total	COMMENTS
Movement Concepts, Personal Space								
A. Execute Body Actions While Standing	"Stretch and curl"				/8		/8	
B. Execute Body Actions While in Prone Position	"Stretch and curl"				/4		/4	
C. Execute Body Actions While in Supine Position	"Stretch and curl"				/4		/4	
D. Move Body Forward and Backward in Space	"Move forward three steps and backward three steps"				/9		/9	
E. Move Body Up and Down in Space	"Move one step up and one step down"				/3		/3	
F. Move Body Sideways in Space	"Move one step left and one step right"				/3		/3	
G. Move Arms Forward and Backward in Space	"Move both arms forward and then backward"				/7		/7	
H. Move Arms Up and Down in Space	"Move both arms up and down"				/7		/7	
I. Move Arms Sideways in Space	"Move both arms sideways from the body"				/3		/3	
J. Move Body Forward and Backward Around Objects in Space	"Move backward and then forward around the chair"				/12		/12	
K. Move Body to Various Positions Around an Object in Space	"Move in front of, to the left side, behind, and to the right side of the chair"				/7		/7	

Figure 4.3. Sample placement form.

MOTOR SKILL SEQUENCE SHEET

LEISURE MOVEMENT

E. Go Down a Slide

Terminal Objective: The student will slide down the slide.

Prerequisite Skills: Climb Stairs

Phase I   The student will sit on the end of the slide and absorb the landing as he gets off.

Phase II   The student will climb the ladder to the top and climb back down.

Phase III   The student will climb the ladder, sit at the top of the slide, and follow the aide down the slide, who reduces the sliding speed.

Phase IV   The student will climb the ladder, sit in front of the aide, and they will slide down together.

Phase V   The student will climb the ladder, sit at the top, and put his soles on the sliding surface to slow down the descent.

Phase VI   The student will slide down the slide.

Program 4

Figure 4.4.   Sample motor skill sequence sheet.

PROGRAM COVER SHEET

Pupil: Jim **Date Started:** April 3, 1985 **Date Completed:**	**Program:** Leisure Skills, E. Go Down a Slide
Verbal Cue: "Jim, slide down the slide."	**Materials:** 1. clipboard 2. pencil 3. slide 4. reinforcer
Instructional Setting: Position Jim so he can see the demonstration.	**Reinforcement Procedure:** Give social reinforcement on completion of task.
Correction: "No, Jim." Model, recue, mild social reinforcement if correct; If not, go to next level of assistance. "No, Jim." Cue. "Jim, slide down the slide." Physically assist Jim as he slides. Socially reinforce on completion of the task.	**Criterion:** Three consecutive correct responses before goint to next step.

Figure 4.5.   Sample program cover sheet (Program 4).

DATA SHEET

Name: Jim   **Program:** Leisure Skills, Go Down a Slide

X = Correct
O = Incorrect

Reinforcer	Phase	Step	Trials 1	2	3	4	5	6	7	8	9	10	Comments	Date
Baseline			VI O/O	V O/X	IV X/X	III X/	II /	I /						4-2 1985
Swing	V		O	O	X	X	O	O	O	X	X	O		4-3 1985
Swing	V		O	O	(X	X	X)							4-4 1985
Swing	VI		O	O	O	X	O	O	X	X	O	O		4-7 1985
Swing	VI		(X	X	X)									4-8 1985
Posttest	VI		X/X											4-9 1985
Maintenance File														4-9 1985

Figure 4.6. Sample data sheet (Program 4).

precise terms how a program is to be conducted. The Program Cover Sheet also helps volunteers to maintain consistency when running a program with a specific student. The verbal cue, for example, has been carefully developed and should be used exactly as written on the sheet. The correction procedure section of the Program Cover Sheet is also very important. For example, if a student fails to respond appropriately to the verbal cue, the volunteer knows that feedback must be given, the skill modeled, and the cue stated again.

The levels of assitance used are generally verbal, model, and physical assistance. It is important to realize that the level of assistance will change from student to student as well as program to program. Some students may start with model then move to physical assistance. Others may use the verbal cue and go directly to physical assistance. The decision to alter the levels of assistance is based on each student's needs. The method that maximizes the student's capability to learn is the one that should be used.

Materials are listed so that the person conducting the program gathers all the necessary equipment, allowing the volunteer to prepare to conduct the program without consulting the teacher. The reinforcers used are taken from the reinforcement file listed on the second page of the clipboard (Figure 4.2). The teacher should continually keep an eye open for items or activities that reinforce the student. Functional reinforcers should be used as often as possible. For example, if the student climbed the ladder to the slide and this was the expected behavior, the teacher could assist the student in sliding down the slide. Listing the reinforcers used helps to ensure consistency in delivering positive reinforcement.

The criterion lets the volunteer know how many successful trials must be performed consecutively before the student can move on to the next phase and/or step. Since the Program Cover Sheet is one-half page, the lower half of the Data Sheet remains visible for easy marking of the data. Figures 4.4, 4.5, and 4.6 are attached to the clipboard so they can be used without flipping pages.

Data Sheet

The Data Sheet, where trial-by-trial data are kept, is a vital component of the clipboard system. Data taken during instruction are recorded after each trial, giving the teacher information on the student's progress. Data are examined daily to determine if a change in a program is necessary. More will be presented in Chapter 6, Keeping Track of Student's Progress, about how to interpret data patterns.

Maintenance File

The final page of the clipboard is the Maintenance File (Figure 4.7). The Maintenance File lists the programs the student has learned, the cues used at the terminal phase and/or step, the terminal objective, the date completed, and the dates to be probed. This form helps to ensure that those programs not naturally falling into a daily routine will be reviewed periodically.

A schematic of the entire clipboard is shown in Figure 4.8

Summary

The Data Based Gymnasium Model was developed to ensure that severely handicapped students receive appropriate instruction. This goal is made possible through the use of the clipboard system. It is really a management system that includes a teacher's blending of the curriculum containing complete scope and sequence, a data-keeping system, materials and reinforcers, aides, volunteers, and parents. Built into the management system is a communication system that allows instructions to be easily delivered to the aides and volunteers, and which provides a feedback channel to the teacher. This system provides the necessary link between the instructional manager, the teacher, volunteers, and aides.

MAINTENANCE FILE

Name _____ Jim _____

PROGRAM: Underhand Strike, Basic Game Skills
Terminal Objective: The student will perform an underhand strike with the preferred arm hitting the ball held with the other hand.
Cue: "Hit the ball underhand."
Date Program Completed: April 1, 1985
Dates to be Probed:

April 15, 1985	X	X	
May 13, 1985	X	X	
June 10, 1985	X	O	X
Sept. 10, 1985	X	X	
Feb. 10, 1986	X	O	O
June 10, 1986			

PROGRAM: Go Down a Slide, Leisure Skills
Terminal Objective: The student will slide down the slide.
Cue: "Jim, slide down the slide."
Date Program Completed: April 9, 1985
Dates to be Probed:

April 23, 1985			
May 21, 1985			
June 25, 1985			
Sept. 22, 1985			
March 23, 1986			
Sept. 22, 1986			

PROGRAM:
Terminal Objective:
Cue:
Date Program Completed: _____
Dates to be Probed: _____

Figure 4.7.   Sample Maintenance File.

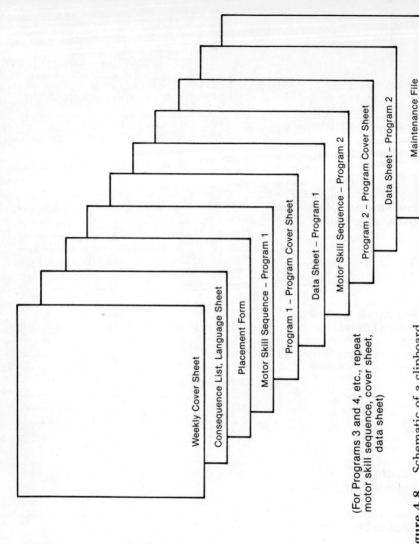

Weekly Cover Sheet

Consequence List, Language Sheet

Placement Form

Motor Skill Sequence – Program 1

Program 1 – Program Cover Sheet

Data Sheet – Program 1

Motor Skill Sequence – Program 2

Program 2 – Program Cover Sheet

Data Sheet – Program 2

Maintenance File

(For Programs 3 and 4, etc., repeat
motor skill sequence, cover sheet,
data sheet)

Figure 4.8. Schematic of a clipboard.

Game, Exercise, and Leisure Sport Curriculum

5

The Game, Exercise, and Leisure Sport curriculum was developed through the joint efforts of staff from the Physical Education Department at Oregon State University (OSU) and staff from the Special Education Department at Teaching Research. Its initial development began in the fall of 1977 when it became apparent that many physical education curricula for the handicapped did not provide adequate programming for the student who was profoundly or severely handicapped. Physical education programs such as Project ACTIVE are quite comprehensive in their scope but are not designed to deal with the student who is severely or profoundly handicapped and are not geared to the low functional levels often found in this population. The sequences in this curriculum are designed to fill that gap.

The initial attempts to develop the sequences were completed by both staffs from OSU and Teaching Research. Placement testing procedures were devised to articulate with the sequences and time was spent testing these sequences on severely and profoundly handicapped students in classrooms at Teaching Research. As a result, several revisions of the curriculum occurred, including extensive field testing of the curriculum items in classrooms other than those at Teaching Research. The curriculum as it now stands has been extensively field tested and has been found effective as a guide for teaching severely handicapped students basic physical education skills. This curriculum will, of course, continue to be revised as more and more teachers have the opportunity to use the curriculum and suggest changes in sequences.

Rationale for the Curriculum

Since the sequences and task analyses in this curriculum take the form of individual prescriptions for the student, it will not be necessary for the teacher to write an individual prescription for each student. It must be emphasized, however, that no curriculum can provide all the needed sequences and task analyses for any particular student. It is the teacher's responsibility to alter the sequences to fit each student's needs. We feel, however, that given this curriculum and the skills to make alterations as necessary, the teacher can provide appropriate game, exercise, and leisure sport experiences for handicapped students.

The curriculum is a series of Motor Skill Sequences (task analyses) of basic physical education skills. The entire concept of task analysis is based on the understanding that, for a student to learn a complex skill, it may be necessary to break down that complex skill into simpler skills and to teach each of those simple skills separately. This curriculum is designed for a program where individual objectives are determined for each student. The procedure of placing each student in the curriculum is described later in this chapter. Once the student is placed in the curriculum, she will be moved through the various behaviors according to priorities established by the teacher and parents or surrogate parents. Each student's progress through the various steps of the curriculum will be tracked with the continuous data system described in Chapter 6. The curriculum is organized into major areas, skills, phases, and steps. This organizational pattern is consistent with others found in Fredericks and the Staff of the Teaching Research Infant and Child Center (1980) and Fredericks, Makohon, Bunse, Buckley, Alrick, and Samples (1980).

Skills, Phases, and Steps

As an example, consider the major area in the curriculum called Basic Game Skills. The second skill in Basic Game Skills is the underhand throw. Within this skill there are six phases (Figure 5.1). The phases are essentially task analyses of the terminal objective listed for the skill of underhand throw. The higher the phase number, the more advanced the skill.

One additional area remains in the curriculum – steps, which are further breakdowns of phase. Steps, for example, may be either differences in length of time, differences in distances, or the number of repetitions required.

Although this curriculum is designed for severely and profoundly handicapped students, teachers with a majority of students who are not handicapped can still use the curriculum as a guide. The detailed breakdown of phases will, however, be unnecessary. For example, in the underhand throw phases of the curriculum it is not necessary to take a nonhandicapped student through each of the phases listed in the underhand throw skill. It is, however, a necessary skill that many students need to practice. For nonhandicapped students the teaching emphasis may be on more precision in form

BASIC GAME SKILLS

B. Underhand Throw

Terminal Objective: The student, standing, will perform an underhand throw swinging the arm backward and then forward while stepping forward simultaneously with the opposite foot and releasing the ball at the end of the swing in a manner which causes the ball to fly in the direction of the target.

Prerequisite Skills: Basic Game Skills A

Phase I   With student standing 5' from target and with knees bent, student will swing arm backward and forward, releasing the ball at end of swing in direction of the target. Teacher assists student in swinging arm back and then forward.

Phase II With student standing 5' from target, teacher assists student in swinging arm back and allows student to swing arm forward independently, releasing ball at target at end of swing.

Phase III With student standing 5' from target, student will independently swing arm backward and forward, releasing ball at end of swing and in direction of target.

Phase IV With student standing 5' from target with one foot forward and one foot back and knees bent, student will swing arm backward and forward, releasing ball at end of swing and in direction of target.

Phase V With student standing 5' from target and with knees bent, student will swing arm backward and forward releasing ball at end of swing and in the direction of the target while teacher is pushing student's *opposite side foot* forward simultaneously with swing.

Phase VI Student, standing, will perform an underhand throw swinging the arm backward and then forward while stepping forward simultaneously with the opposite foot and releasing the ball at the end of the swing in a manner which causes the ball to fly in direction of the target.

The following steps apply to Phase VI.

Steps:

1. 7'
2. 12'

Suggested Materials: Tennis ball and 3' by 3' target placed on the floor.

Teaching Notes: 1. For those students in wheelchairs, the underhand throw can be performed with the student sitting in the wheelchair, thus eliminating the need for Phases IV-VI.

2. For nonambulatory students who are not in a wheelchair, ball throwing can be taught from a supported sitting position.

Figure 5.1. Underhand throw.

and accuracy. The teacher who uses this curriculum should always strive to have the student accomplish the terminal objective in the skill before attempting to teach the phases. There is no need to move every student through the curriculum step by step, phase by phase. The student's movement through the curriculum should be dependent upon her motor ability and the rate at which she can acquire motor skills.

Branching

On the other end of the continuum, of course, is the student who is so severely and profoundly handicapped that the task analyses for some sequences provided in this curriculum still do not provide small enough steps or phases. In these instances, it is necessary to engage in branching, breaking a task down into easier increments. For example, for a student having difficulty in moving from Phase IV to Phase V in the skill of striking, the teacher merely changes the amount or type of assistance. If that is too large a move for some students, the program has to be branched. In this case, the teacher writes Phase Va which might indicate that the teacher assists by holding the student's arm three-quarters of the way down rather than at the elbow. Thus when the student is able to meet criterion at this phase, the teacher can move to Phase V, which is placing one hand on the student's elbow. Despite the fact that branching programs may at times be necessary for certain students, the basic curriculum provides a good foundation for them. Usually, only a few branching steps need to be written and added to an existing program to make it a suitable program for even the most severely handicapped student. This maintains one of the main purposes of the curriculum, which is to save the teacher time.

Remember that many of the skills in the curriculum may be taught simultaneously. A teacher with a severely and profoundly handicapped student may be teaching skills and sequences in the areas of movement concepts, games, and physical fitness at the same time. It is our experience that the teacher will have a particular student on three to five physical education programs at the same time.

Placement Testing

Placement testing is the initial testing procedure used. It is the assessment given on a series of skills to determine the specific motor skills a student already has and those not yet acquired. This assessment process tests the highest level of each skill in the curriculum, but it does not test each specific phase or part of the skill. In other words, it is a gross assessment of a student's skills and involves making a yes or no judgment.

Prior to testing, the teacher should spend time observing the student's motor behavior patterns. The preferred hand and foot should be determined by setting up a play environment which brings about motor responses that give this type of information. During this observation time, items that appear to be reinforcing to the student should be noted. They can be used later during one-to-one instruction and should be recorded on page 2 of the clipboard. Discussions with those who know the student will also give the teacher some idea of beneficial skills.

After the skills to be tested have been listed, the teacher prepares for the placement session. The skills to be placed should be marked with an asterisk (*) in the skill column of the Placement Form. All necessary equipment is gathered along with the clipboard and Placement Form.

Placement Form

The Placement Form, Figure 5.2, is designed to facilitate the data-keeping process. The first column lists all the skills in order they are presented in the curriculum. The cue listed need not be used if it is incongruent with the student's receptive language level. Any cue change, however, should be recorded under the cue column. The month, day, and year need to be recorded in the date column. The placement data are recorded in the next column.

The teacher tests the student at the terminal objective of the skill. At least two trials are given for each skill tested. A third trial may be administered if the student performs one correct trial and one incorrect trial. A "yes" is recorded if the student scores correctly on two out of three trials. A "no" is recorded if the student scores two out of three incorrectly. The student should be reinforced for appropriate social behavior. Reinforcement for correct motor performance is not permitted. The teacher must model the appropriate motor response each time the student is cued to perform a new task.

When the student is successful on a particular skill, the teacher should add the skill to the student's Maintenance File and periodically check to see if the skill has been retained. If the skill is used in the student's daily activities, there is no need to place it in the Maintenance File.

When the placement testing is completed, the test results are shared with the parents and a decision is made as to which skills are priority items. These skills are then included on the student's individualized educational plan.

PLACEMENT FORM

For all skills listed below, cue by saying, "Watch me," demonstrate, and then use verbal and/or signed cue listed below.

SKILL	CUE	DATE	Placement Yes/No	DATE	Baseline #/Total	DATE	Posttest #/Total	Comments
B. Underhand Throw *	"Throw the ball underhand at the target."	10-8 1985	OXO No	10-9 1985	2/7	10-20 1985	7/7	
C. Overhand Throw *	"Throw the ball underhand at the target."	10-8 1985	XOX Yes		/7		/7	
D. Underhand Strike *	"Hit the ball underhand."	10-8 1985	OO No	10-9 1985	4/7		/7	
E. Overhand Strike	"Hit the ball overhand."				/8		/8	
F. Kicking With the Toe, Preferred Foot	"Kick the ball with your toe."				/7		/7	
G. Kicking With the Toe, Nonpreferred Foot	"Kick the ball with your toe using the other foot."				/7		/7	
H. Kicking With the Instep, Preferred Foot	"Kick the ball with your instep."				/7		/7	
I. Kicking With the Instep, Nonpreferred Foot	"Kick the ball with the instep of your other foot."				/7		/7	
J. Kicking With the Side of the Foot, Preferred Foot	"Kick the ball with the side of your foot."				/7		/7	
K. Kicking With the Side of the Foot, Nonpreferred Foot	"Kick the ball with the side of your other foot."				/7		/7	
L. Trapping or Catching a Rolled Ball	"Stop the ball."				/5		/5	
M. Catching a Bouncing Ball	"Catch the ball."				/5		/5	
N. Catching a Thrown Ball	"Catch the ball."				/14		/14	

Figure 5.2. Sample placement form.

Baseline Data Sheet

When placement is complete and program priorities have been established, the teacher begins the baseline procedures. Baselining is a process by which the teacher pinpoints specifically which phases and steps within each skill the student does or does not have. An accurate place to begin teaching a particular skill is thus determined.

The materials needed should be gathered prior to baselining. There should be a Placement Form, Motor Behavior Sequence Sheet for each skill, Program Cover Sheet, and a Data Sheet for each skill tested. These forms should be added to the clipboard prior to testing.

The baseline Data Sheet must be completed for each program being baselined. The teacher should determine how many phases and steps there are for the program to be baselined and to which phases the steps belong. For example, there are six phases and two steps for Phase VI on the underhand throw. The baseline Data Sheet for the underhand throw is illustrated in Figure 5.3.

As indicated in Figure 5.3, the student's name and the motor skill are recorded on the appropriate lines. For the underhand throw, the phases (VI to I) are listed in reverse order. Phase VI has two steps but the other phases have only one step.

The baseline procedure is very similar to the placement process. The motor task is modeled before the cue is given. The cue used is task specific and appropriate for the student's receptive language level. Two trials are given for each phase. The baseline procedure begins at the highest phase and step, and works to the easiest phase or until the student performs correctly at any one phase and/or step. When this occurs, the teacher should update the clipboard and begin 1:1 instruction at the next highest phase or step (Figure 5.4).

When baselining it is important not to reinforce the student for performing a motor skill correctly. Reinforcement should be given only for appropriate social behavior. Physical assistance or any form of correction should not be used unless it is written into the task analysis.

Bracketing.   If it becomes apparent when conducting a baseline that the student will have difficulty completing the higher phases and/or steps of a skill, the teacher may elect to skip higher phases of the skill and move directly to the lower phases. Bracketing is the term used to refer to this process.

DATA SHEET

Name: Jim   **Program:** _____ Underhand Throw

X = Correct
O = Incorrect

Reinforcer	Phase	Step	Trials 1	2	3	4	5	6	7	8	9	10	Comments	Date
Baseline	VI	1-2	VI	V	IV	III	II	I						
		1	/	/	/	/	/	/						
		2	/											

Figure 5.3. Sample baseline data sheet for underhand throw.

DATA SHEET

Name: Jim   Program: _____ Underhand Throw

X = Correct
O = Incorrect

Reinforcer	Phase	Step	Trials 1	2	3	4	5	6	7	8	9	10	Comments	Date
Baseline	VI / V-I	1-2	VI	V	IV	III	II	I						
		1	X	X	X	O/X	X/X	/						
	III	2	O/O											

Figure 5.4. Bracketing a skill.

In physical education some motor skill sequences are considered cumulative; that is, a student who performs a skill within a motor sequence is considered to have acquired all the skills or phases prior to the one just performed. Thus, there is no need to test any of the preceding skills in the sequence. The baseline procedure for these is the same as mentioned above.

Other skills in the *Game, Exercise, and Leisure Sport Curriculum* are considered noncumulative. This means that there is very little transfer of skill ability from one phase to another within the same task analysis. The assumption cannot be made that if one phase is performed, preceding skills can be done correctly. Each phase must be tested as a separate entity.

The final step in the baseline process is to record the entry level skill on the Placement Form in the baseline column. As indicated on the Placement Form (Figure 5.2), Jim failed the placement test for the underhand throw. When this information was shared with the IEP team, a decision was made to include this skill in Jim's program. The skill was then baselined and the results were recorded in the baseline column. The number printed as a denominator denotes the total number of phases and steps in the task analysis for the underhand throw. The numerator is the number of phases and steps the student can perform correctly. Assuming the skill is cumulative, Jim's score is 2, since this is the total number of phases and steps Jim performed successfully during the baseline procedure.

The baseline data should always be kept with the program so that it may be referred to during the updating process. The baseline data informs the teacher of the student's entry level skill and of skills learned since that time. The baseline information should be added to the Placement Form as illustrated in Figure 5.2.

Posttesting.   After the student has met criterion at the final phase and/or step, a posttest is given the following day to ensure skill maintenance. Two trials are administered at the highest phase using the same cueing process used during one-to-one instruction. For example, if the student has a low receptive language level, the model is performed first, then the cue is given. Strong reinforcement is used for appropriate attending behaviors. A neutral social reinforcer is used for appropriate motor responses during the posttest (e.g., "Thank you").

When postesting a cumulative skill, only the terminal objective (highest phase/step) should be tested (see Figure 5.5). When posttesting a noncumulativae skill, each phase and step must be tested unless the terminal objective incorporates all components of the motor skill (see Figure 5.6).

DATA SHEET

X = Correct
O = Incorrect

Name: ___Jim___

Program: ___Underhand Throw___

Reinforcer	Phase	Step	Trials											Comments	Date
			1	2	3	4	5	6	7	8	9	10		
1:1 Social	VI	2	O	X	X	X								10-18 1985
Posttest	VI	2	X/X											10-19 1985

Figure 5.5. Posttesting a cumulative skill.

DATA SHEET

X = Correct
O = Incorrect

Name: ___Jim___   Program: _____   Three Part Body Movement

Reinforcer	Phase	Step	Trials										Comments	Date
			1	2	3	4	5	6	7	8	9	10		
1:1 Social	III		O	X	O	X	X	X						10-18 1985
			III	II	I									
Posttest			X/X	X/X	X/X									10-19 1985

Figure 5.6. Posttesting a noncumulative skill.

If the results of the posttest are positive, the posttest total should be recorded under the posttest column on the Placement Form. The date of completion should be recorded on the Placement Form as well as on the Program Cover Sheet (see Figure 5.2). The skill should then be placed in the Maintenance File.

Maintenance File

A Maintenance File is established when the posttest results are positive. It should be completed as shown in Figure 5.7. The purpose of the file is to determine whether or not the skill will be retained. The maintenance schedule should be individualized and reflect the student's ability to retain a skill. A traditional maintenance schedule checks for retention two weeks, one month, two months, three months, and six months after completion of the program. The time frame may need to be altered on occasion because of the various demands put upon the teacher.

Not all programs need to be placed on a maintenance schedule. Functional skills used in a daily living routine need not be included on the file. For example, when a student who has learned to swing uses the swing during recess, there is no need to test the child on swinging.

Reinforcement Procedures

The procedures for reinforcement during a placement test and baseline are the same. Primary/tangible and/or social reinforcers are delivered throughout the placement test contingent upon appropriate behaviors such as attending to a task, maintaining eye contact, waiting patiently, and following commands not related to the task being tested (e.g., "Come here," "Sit down," "Give me the toy"). Reinforcers are *not* delivered contingent upon correct performance on the specific test items. The rationale for this procedure is that delivery of reinforcers contingent upon correct performance constitutes treatment or teaching. On the other hand, the placement and baseline (pretest) constitute evaluation of the student's performance prior to treatment. During these tests, however, reinforcers are delivered in order to maintain those behaviors (e.g., attention to task, sitting, waiting) necessary for a smooth and pleasant testing situation, and to keep the student motivated to continue attempting new tasks.

The frequency with which reinforcers are delivered is individual to each student. The profoundly handicapped student may require primary and social reinforcement at a high rate (every 15 seconds) while the moderately handicapped adolescent may work for the en-

MAINTENANCE FILE

Name _____Jim_____

PROGRAM: Underhand Throw
Terminal Objective: The student, standing, will perform an underhand throw swinging the arm backward and then forward while stepping forward simultaneously with the opposite foot and releasing the ball at the end of the swing in a manner which causes the ball to fly in the direction of the target.
Cue: "Throw the ball underhand at the target."

Date Program Completed:	Oct. 18, 1985			
Dates to be Probed:	Nov. 2, 1985			
	Dec. 2, 1985			
	Jan. 2, 1986			
	April 2, 1986			
	Oct. 1, 1986			
	April 2, 1986			

PROGRAM:
Terminal Objective:
Cue:
Date Program Completed: _____
Dates to be Probed: _____

PROGRAM:
Terminal Objective:
Cue:
Date Program Completed: _____
Dates to be Probed: _____

Figure 5.7.   Sample Maintenance File.

tire placement test session given only periodic social praise and a free time break after 30 minutes as a reward. Again, the teacher can determine the frequency of reinforcement through information gathered from parents, former teachers, and through her own informal observations prior to the placement test.

Individual Education Program (IEP)

After placement testing the student, the teacher develops the student's Individual Education Program (IEP) with the parents and appropriate school personnel. The IEP, with its long- and short-range goals, provides the basis for the programs that are eventually placed on the clipboard. An example of a student's physical education IEP is shown in Figure 5.8.

INDIVIDUAL EDUCATION PROGRAM

Name Jim

Priorities of Long-range Objectives
1. Jim will strike a ball with an underhand motion.
2. Jim will catch a ball.
3. Jim will kick a ball with the toe.
4. Jim will run 300 yards without stopping.
5. Jim will go down a slide.
6.
7.
8.
9.
10.

I have examined my child's Individual Education Program, including the priorities of long-range objectives, short-range objectives for each long-range objective as shown in the attached sheets, and baseline and progress data.

Date: Signature:

Figure 5.8. Sample IEP.

Short-range Objectives	Home	1:1	Group	Baseline		Review		Review		Revisions		Maintenance		Comments
				Date	Data	Date	Data	Date	Data	Date	Change	Date	Status	
1. Bring the arm backward and then forward striking the ball in the direction of the target with teacher assistance.														
2. Strike the ball underhand in the direction of a target 5' away.														
3. Strike the ball underhand with one foot in front of the other (opposition) at a target 10' away.														
4. Strike the ball underhand while stepping with the opposite foot.														

I have examined my child's Individual Education Plan including the priorities of long-range goals and short-range objectives. In reviewing the plan I have also examined the baseline and progress data.

Date: _____

Signature: _____

Figure 5.8. Continued.

Priority # 2   Long-range Goal: Jim _____ will increase and/or develop his/her skills in the area of _____ Physical Education _____.

Short-range Objectives	Home	1:1	Group	Baseline Date	Baseline Data	Review Date	Review Data	Review Date	Review Data	Revisions Date	Revisions Change	Maintenance Date	Maintenance Status	Comments
1. Jim will catch an 8" ball thrown from 2 feet away with teacher assistance.														
2. Jim will catch an 8" ball thrown from a distance of 4 feet.														
3. Jim will catch a tennis ball thrown from a distance of 4 feet.														
4. Jim will catch a tennis ball thrown from a distance of 8 feet within a one stride distance to Jim's left or right.														

I have examined my child's Individual Education Plan including the priorities of long-range goals and short-range objectives. In reviewing the plan I have also examined the baseline and progress data.

Date: _____

Signature: _____
_____
_____

Figure 5.8. Continued.

Priority # 3   Long-range Goal: Jim _____ will increase and/or develop his/her skills in the area of ___ Physical Education ___.

Short-range Objectives	Home	1:1	Group	Baseline Date	Baseline Data	Review Date	Review Data	Review Date	Review Data	Revisions Date	Revisions Change	Maintenance Date	Maintenance Status	Comments
1. Jim will kick a ball 5 feet with the toe with teacher assistance.														
2. Jim will kick a ball 10 feet with the toe with teacher prompting.														
3. Jim will kick a ball with the toe 10 feet.														
4. Jim will kick a ball with the toe 20 feet to a target.														

I have examined my child's Individual Education Plan including the priorities of long-range goals and short-range objectives. In reviewing the plan I have also examined the baseline and progress data.

Date: _____

Signature: _____

Figure 5.8. Continued.

Priority # 4   Long-range Goal: Jim _____ will increase and/or develop his/her skills in the area of ___ Physical Education ___.

Short-range Objectives	Home	1:1	Group	Baseline		Review		Review		Revisions		Maintenance		Comments
				Date	Data	Date	Data	Date	Data	Date	Change	Date	Status	
1. Jim will walk 100 yards without stopping.														
2. Jim will run 25 yards without stopping.														
3. Jim will run 50 yards without stopping.														
4. Jim will run 100 yards without stopping.														
5. Jim will run 200 yards without stopping.														
6. Jim will run 300 yards without stopping.														

I have examined my child's Individual Education Plan including the priorities of long-range goals and short-range objectives. In reviewing the plan I have also examined the baseline and progress data.

Date: _____

Signature: _____
_____
_____

Figure 5.8. Continued.

Keeping Track of Student Progress 6

In order to provide efficient individual programming, a teacher must be able to measure accurately the student's skills and capabilities in all curricular areas. The teacher must further be able to track the student's progress through the curricular areas. Implied in this tracking procedure is the necessity to respond to the data collected. For instance, if a volunteer is instructing a student in a particular physical education program and the data on the student's progress indicate that no progress has been made for the past two days, the teacher should observe the program being run. If it appears that the instructional mechanics are in place, then the teacher is required under the system outlined in this chapter to modify the student's program by reducing the complexity of the task, increasing the power of the reinforcer, or by modifying the way the materials are presented to the student.

On the other hand, if the student is moving rapidly through the steps of a sequence with few incorrect responses, the teacher should probe ahead to determine whether the student possesses more advanced skills that would allow him to move through the sequence more rapidly or to skip portions of the instructional sequence.

Thus, in both instances the data are telling the physical education teacher to alter the student's program. The ability to respond to the data and to modify programs accordingly is the essence of individual programming. Therefore, to function effectively in this system, physical education teachers must be able to make as accurate an initial assessment as possible of the student's motor capabilities, place the student in the scope and sequence of the curriculum, and maintain data on student progress so as to modify programs when needed.

In addition, the physical education teacher must be prepared to inaugurate programs to measure and change social behaviors that interfere with the learning process – tantrumming, crying, aggressive behavior, noncompliance, etc.

Chapter 5 discussed the initial assessment of a student in the curriculum; Chapter 3 discussed the assessment of the student in social programs. This chapter is devoted to those elements designed to keep track of a student's progress in the acquisition of skills after the initial assessment.

Tracking Skill Acquisition Programs

After the initial assessment has been made in a curricular area, the teacher is ready to begin the student's instructional program. This, of course, assumes that there are no social behaviors that will interfere with the instructional program and prevent learning from occurring. If there are such behaviors, they should be treated first.

The following is an example of a student, Jim, who does not have such behaviors and who has been placed in a program for kicking with the preferred foot. The phases and steps that the student will go through are shown in Figure 6.1. The program, to be conducted daily, is described on a Program Cover Sheet (Figure 6.2).

Updating

All data for the acquisition of skills are recorded after each trial. We believe that this ensures the most efficient teaching. A moderately or severely handicapped student, by the nature of his handicap, will be retarded in the acquisition of many skills. His educators have a responsibility to do everything they can to offset the effects of the handicap by providing the student with as many skills as possible through appropriate teaching.

If teachers do not help the student to learn at this optimum growth rate, they are in fact further contributing to his retardation. The purpose of the continuous data system, therefore, is to give immediate (daily) feedback so teaching modifications can be made in a timely fashion, optimizing the student's rate of learning. Thus, data are examined daily, usually after instruction hours, to determine if a change in a program is necessary. This process of examining data, decisions about change, and recording the program for the next day is called updating.

The purpose of collecting data and reviewing the program daily is to provide ample information for making appropriate programming decisions. Reviewing the following items will give a more complete picture of the student's progress and may provide a better insight into what alterations are needed:

BASIC GAME SKILLS

F. Kicking With the Toe, Preferred Foot

Terminal Objective: Student, from a standing position, will perform a kick by swinging the preferred leg backwards and then forwards, striking the ball with the toe of the foot, causing the ball to roll in the direction of a target.

Prerequisite Skills: Fine Motor Skills — Lower Extremity, K.

Phase I Student, from a standing position, will perform a kick by swinging the preferred leg backwards and then forwards, striking the ball with the toe of the foot, causing the ball to roll in the direction of a target placed 5 feet away. The teacher will assist the child by placing her hand on his preferred leg and pushing the leg backwards and then forwards, causing it to strike the ball with the toe of the foot.

Phase II Student, from a standing position, will perform a kick by swinging the preferred leg backwards and then forwards, striking the ball with the toe of the foot, causing the ball to roll in the direction of a target placed 5 feet away. The teacher will assist the child by placing her hand on the child's preferred leg, and forcing the leg backwards and prompting it forwards, allowing the leg to strike the ball with the toe of the foot.

Phase III Student, from a standing position, will perform a kick by swinging the preferred leg backwards and then forward, striking the ball with the toe of the foot, causing the ball to roll in the direction of the target placed 5 feet away. The teacher will assist the student by placing her hand on the preferred leg and forcing the leg backwards, allowing the leg to come forward and strike the ball on the toe.

Phase IV · Student, from a standing position, will perform a kick by swinging the preferred leg backwards and then forwards, striking the ball with the toe of the foot, causing the ball to roll in the direction of the target placed 5 feet away. The teacher will assist the student by placing her hand on the student's preferred leg and prompting the foot backwards, allowing the leg to then come forward and strike the ball on the toe of the foot.

Phase V Student, from a standing position, will perform a kick by swinging the preferred leg backwards and then forwards, striking the ball with the toe of the foot, causing the ball to roll in the direction of the target.

The following steps apply to Phase V.

Steps:

1. 10'
2. 15'
3. 20'

Suggested Materials: An 8" diameter rubber ball.

Figure 6.1. Kicking with the toe, preferred foot.

PROGRAM COVER SHEET

Pupil: Jim **Date Started:** 3/3 **Date Completed:**	**Program:** Kicking with Preferred Foot
Verbal Cue: "Jim, kick the ball."	**Materials:** Ball 8" to 10" in diameter, area 20' long
Instructional Setting: Place ball in front of child. Point to the target. Be sure Jim is attending before you cue him.	**Reinforcement Procedure:** 1:1 Social Pair social with mini-jogger
Correction: "No, Jim. Watch." (Teacher demonstrates) Recue. "Jim, kick the ball." (If correct, mildly reinforce.) "No, Jim. Kick the ball at the target." Physically assist and socially reinforce.	**Criterion:** Three consecutive correct responses

Figure 6.2. Program cover sheet for Jim.

1. Review the phases and steps of the task analysis.
2. Check the criterion for advancement (program cover sheet).
3. Check the phase and step the student is on (data sheet).
4. Check the comments section next to the day's data (data sheet).
5. Check the data pattern on the data sheet.
6. Check the baseline (data sheet) to determine which steps the student has already learned.
7. If there is some confusion about the program update, check to see if a program is being updated from a probe.

There are six possible major decisions a teacher may make about a program during the updating process:

1. Maintain the program as is.
2. Probe ahead to determine if the student can perform at a more

advanced step of the program.

3. Change the reinforcer being used with the program.
4. Branch the program to add additional steps that will either make the task easier or will provide additional support to the student while performing the task.
5. Probe backward to determine that the student has mastered previous steps.
6. Temporarily cancel the program.

The data pattern plus knowledge about the student's previous performance dictates which of the above decisions the teacher will make during the updating process. A discussion of each follows:

Maintain the Program. If a student is progressing satisfactorily in a program, the teacher will decide to continue that program as is during the next class day. A number of data patterns for a particular program will elicit this decision. Figure 6.3 shows a pattern where the student has reached criterion (three consecutive correct responses) for a step in the program. The update for that program is merely designating the next step in the program. This is shown for 2/6 (February 6) in Figure 6.3. Notice that the teacher has not specified the reinforcer to be used for the next day. This lack of specification means that the volunteer has the option of selecting a reinforcer from the student's consequence file.

Figure 6.4 presents a different data pattern. It is obvious from this pattern that the student has had intermittent success throughout the day (2/6). Since she has been working on this step fo theprogram for only one day, the teacher's decision is to maintain the program for another day. The updating decision as recorded on the data sheet appears in Figure 6.4. Again, there is no need at this time to specify a reinforcement change.

Probe Ahead. Students occasionally progress through programs at a much faster pace that expected. This rapid progress usually occurs for several reasons: 1) the student initially was assessed erroneously in the program; 2) after the student has acquired the initial steps of a program, the remaining steps, which are extensions of the initial steps, are more easily acquired by some students; and 3) the student's developmental patterns parallel the presentation of some skills (i.e., he is ready to learn the new skill). Al pattern of data indicating this phenomenon appears in Figure 6.5. Therefore, the teacher's decision is to probe ahead.

DATA SHEET

X = Correct
O = Incorrect

Name: Jim

Program: Kick with Preferred Foot

Reinforcer	Phase	Step	Trials 1	2	3	4	5	6	7	8	9	10	Comments	Date
1:1 Social	II		O	X	O	X	X	X						2-5 1985
1:1 Social	III													2-6 1985

Figure 6.3. Update for the above data pattern.

DATA SHEET

X = Correct
O = Incorrect

Name: ___Jim___

Program: ___Kick with Preferred Foot___

Reinforcer	Phase	Step	Trials										Comments	Date
			1	2	3	4	5	6	7	8	9	10		
1:1 Social	III		X	O	O	X	O	X	O	O	O	X		2-6 1985
1:1 Social	III													2-7 1985

Figure 6.4. Data pattern for maintaining the program.

DATA SHEET

X = Correct
O = Incorrect

Name: Jim   Program: Kick with Preferred Foot

Reinforcer	Phase	Step	1	2	3	4	5	6	7	8	9	10	Comments	Date
						Trials								
1:1 Social	III		O	X	O	X	X	X						2-7 1985
	IV		X	O	X	X	X							2-8 1985
	V	1	X	X	X									2-9 1985
			V											
Probe Ahead		2	/											
		3	/											2-10 1985

Figure 6.5. Data pattern which suggests probing ahead.

When a student performs very well, the teacher validates the success by probing ahead to the final phase to determine if the skill has already been mastered. The probe in Figure 6.5 uses two trials with the same reinforcers and schedule as those used during one-to-one instruction. If on 2/10 the student succeeded in both trialls at Steps 2 and 3, a posttest would be administered. However, if the student failed at V-3 and was successful at V-2, programming would be continued at V-3.

Conducting a probe is very similar to baselining, with the exception that the tangible reinforcer is paired with social praise when a student performs correctly. No physical assistance is used unless it is written into the task analysis.

Change the Reinforcer. Figure 6.6 shows data fora two-day period during which the student exhibited intermittent success. Such a pattern indicates that the behavior is within the student's capability, but that the student perhaps needs a greater incentive to perform the motor skill consistently. After noticing this data pattern, the teacher should observe the program being run. If the student continues to have problems, a probe back to ensure that the skill has been maintained at the previous phase may be in order. When the student experiences occasional success, but appears to lack motivation, the general assumption is that the reinforcer is inadequate. The recommendation would be to conduct the program at the same phase and step, but use a stronger, more appropriate reinforcer. This change should be recorded in the reinforcement column and on the daily cover sheet, a decision reflected in Figure 6.6. In this case the reinforcer, jumping on the mini-jogger, is designated by the teacher for use in tomorrow's lesson. Thus, the volunteer is not permitted to choose the reinforcer.

Branch the Program. When a student experiences difficulty for two days on a particular motor task and the teacher has observed the program being run, a probe back is done. When program mechanics and reinforcement changes have been ruled out and the previous phase has been maintained, a branch or program change is in order (see Figure 6.7). Branching usually occurs in one of two ways:

1. Adding steps to make the behavior less difficult. For instance, if Step 2 of a motor sequence required a student to kick a ball for 15 feet and Step 3 required the student to kick the ball for 20 feet, and if the student was able to accomplish Step 2 but not Step 3, a branch might be indicated. The branch could reduce the distance of the kick by adding steps as follows:

DATA SHEET

Name: ___Jim___   Program: ___Kick with Preferred Foot___

X = Correct
O = Incorrect

Reinforcer	Phase	Step	Trials 1	2	3	4	5	6	7	8	9	10	Comments	Date
1:1 Social	IV	2	O	X	O	X	O	X	O	O	X	O		2-8 1985
1:1 Social	IV	2	X	O	X	X	O	X	O	X	X	O		2-9 1985
		IV												
Probe Back		1	X/X										Change reinforcer	2-10 1985
1:1 Social Mini-Jogger	IV	2												

Figure 6.6. Data pattern showing intermittent success suggests a change of reinforcer.

DATA SHEET

X = Correct
O = Incorrect

Name: Jim

Program: Kick with Preferred Foot

Reinforcer	Phase	Step	Trials 1	2	3	4	5	6	7	8	9	10	Comments	Date
1:1 Social	V	1	O	O	O	O	O	O	O	O	O	O		2-13 1985
Mini-Jogger			O	O	O	O	O	O	O	O	O	O		2-14 1985
			IV											
Probe Back		1	/											
		2	/											
		3	/											
		4	X/X											
	V	1a												

Figure 6.7. Data pattern suggests that the program is too difficult and indicates a need to branch.

Original Sequence	Branch
2. 15 feet	3a. 19 feet
3. 20 feet	3b. 18 feet
	3c. 17 feet
	3d. 16 feet

2. Adding additional cues by providing additional nonverbal support. For instance, a student is in a kicking with preferred foot program and is at Phase IV, which is described below:

Phase IV. Student, from standing position, will perform a kick by swinging the preferred leg backwards and then forwards, striking the ball with the toe of the foot, causing the ball to roll in the direction of the target placed 5 feet away. The teacher will assist the student by placing her hand on the student's preferred leg and prompting the foot backwards, allowing the leg to then come forward and strike the ball on the toe of the foot.

Step 1. Trainer delivers verbal cue.

The student is successful at Phase IV of the Kicking with Preferred Foot Program. However, at Phase V, Step 1, the data resemble those appearing in Figure 6.7 on 2/13 and 2/14.

Phase V. Student, from standing position, will perform a kick by swinging the preferred leg backwards and then forwards, striking the ball with the toe of the foot, causing the ball to roll in the direction of the target.

Step 1. 10 feet.

The teacher decides to branch the program, which appears on the behavior sequence sheet as follows:

1a. Prompt the foot at calf with verbal cue.
1b. Push the foot at calf with verbal cue.
1c. Push the foot of the student with verbal cue.

Branches can appear not only as physical assists but also as variations of verbal cues or combinations of the two.

In a branch such as those just described, updating the clipboard requires entries in two places. First, modify the behavioral sequence sheet by writing in the necessary additional steps. The volunteer who will teach the program is cued to refer to the behavioral sequence sheet by the second entry on the Data Sheet, shown in Figure 6.8. The subletter added to the step indicates that the program has been branched.

Another of the teacher's considerations when branching a program is that the reinforcer to be used should be the most powerful available for the student. Although the data pattern may indicate branching, these patterns can only be considered as clues to efficient programming. They are not fool-proof indicators. Therefore, prudence dictates that a teacher faced with data indicating poor or no performance should use the most powerful reinforcement prior to branching the program.

There is one other type of branching to be considered. The teacher may determine that materials used in the program are inadequate and others may be more suitable for a particular student. Therefore, the teacher may choose to revise the program based on the new materials. For example, the teacher may use a ball of a different size, color, or texture. Such changes require nothing more than a notation on the individual cover sheet, but it might also require changing the behavioral sequence sheet. The teacher may also change the type of verbal or visual cue being presented to the student.

Probe Backward. When faced with the possibility of branching, the teacher must make certain considerations. There is the possibility that the student's poor performance may be due to erroneous data previous step be probed to ensure that the student is able to accomplish it. If the student can demonstrate in the probe that he can perform the previous step, the branching technique is warranted. If he cannot, he will have to be placed in the program where he can accomplish the step.

There may be reasons other than erroneous data for a student being unable to perform the previous step of the program. The criterion level for moving to the next step may be set too low for overlearning to occur, and the student may subsequently "forget" the skill he learned on the previous day. If this phenomenon occurs more than once in a particular curricular area, the criterion for moving to the next step should be raised. For instance, if the criterion has been three consecutive responses before moving to the next step, it probably should be raised to four consecutive responses. This type of updating requires a change on the individual program sheet.

DATA SHEET

Name: ___Jim___

X = Correct
O = Incorrect

Reinforcer	Phase	Step	1	2	3	4	5	6	7	8	9	10	Comments	Date
								Trials						
Social	V	3	O	O	O	X	O	O	O	O	O	O		2-5 1985
Social	V	3	O	O	O	O	O	O	O	O	O	O		2-6 1985
Probe Back			V											
		1	/											
		2	X/X											
Social	V	3a											Kick from 19 feet	

Figure 6.8. Update showing decision to branch.

Temporarily Cancel the Program. If a program is not succeeding and the teacher has used all the most powerful reinforcers known and has branched the program in as many ways as can be determined, the program should not be continued. Cancelling a program is an appropriate educational decision when the teacher has exhausted the modifications available. To keep the student in the program at that point would only lmaintain the student in a failure situation. Therefore, it is better to cancel the program, and return to the cancelled program at a future time.

Maintenance System

A Maintenance File is established when the posttest results are positive. The purpose of the file is to determine whether or not the skill has been retained over various retention intervals. The schedule should be child centered and reflect the student's ability to retain a skill.

Formal maintenance programs are established only for those skills not used periodically at home or at school. Any skill that is functional and part of the student's daily routine need not be put on any formal maintenance schedule. However, certain skills are discrete. The vast majority of these are the terminal objectives of cumulative skills. Catching a ball is such a skill. Unless the student is engaging in a sport that allows continuous practice with such a skill, proficiency in the skill can decrease and must be periodically probed to determine if additional practice or instruction is necessary. In these cases the skill seldom disappears, but the performance level may decrease. In catching a ball or hitting a ball with any bat, club, or racquet, the number of misses may have increased with lack of practice. Skills that require stamina, strength, or speed may also have diminished and may also have to be probed to determine the level of maintenance. Figure 6.9 shows a partially completed Maintenance File.

The teacher runs two trails, entering data in the available spaces. If one trial is correct and one trial is incorrect, a third trial is run and the data is entered. The first probe is run two weeks after completion of the program. The second and third probes are run at one-month intervals. The fourth probe is run three months later, with the fifth and sixth probes being run in six-month intervals. If the data indicate the skill is maintained to this point, it is considered part of the student's repertoire.

The program sheets for programs on maintenance are on one

MAINTENANCE FILE

Name _Jim_

PROGRAM: Catches ball
Terminal Objective: Child catches ball at 20.′
Cue: "Catch the ball."
Date Program Completed: Oct. 5, 1983
Dates to be Probed:

Oct. 19, 1983			
Nov. 19, 1983			
Dec. 19, 1983			
March 19, 1984			
Sept. 19, 1984			
March 19, 1985			

PROGRAM: Runs 440 yards
Terminal Objective: 440 yards in 180 seconds.
Cue: "Run."
Date Program Completed: Aug. 7, 1984
Dates to be Probed:

Aug. 21, 1984			
Sept. 21, 1984			
Oct. 21, 1984			
Jan. 21, 1985			
June 21, 1985			
Jan. 21, 1986			

PROGRAM:
Terminal Objective:
Cue:
Date Program Completed: _____
Dates to be Probed:

Figure 6.9. Sample Maintenance File.

clipboard for volunteer use. The volunteer is to pull this sheet, which is listed in alphabetical order, before running the program. It will provide any additional information not included on the Maintenance File. At the end of the week, when the percentage gains form is completed, a check is made to assure that a probe date has not been missed. If it has, a new date is entered on the Maintenance File and a note made for staff to make sure the second date is not missed.

Volunteers: Training and Use 7

The means of providing individual physical education programs is usually not difficult for mildly handicapped students. Many individualized basic game skills or physical fitness activities can include a self-recording technique to assist students in achieving weekly goals. However, with more severely handicapped or younger students, the problem of individual programming becomes not only one of structuring activities in sequence but of providing a one-to-one teacher/pupil relationship. In these instances, the use of aides and volunteers is almost mandatory.

Although an aide may be hired to provide assistance, one person does not allow for extensive individualized instruction and, generally, additional volunteer assistance is needed.

Another reason for including volunteers in the classroom stems from the study conducted by Fredericks et al. (1977), which identified indicators of competencies in teachers of the severely handicapped. The primary indicator was the teacher's ability to maximize instructional time. One method of maximizing this time found in classrooms where students were making high gains was the use of volunteers to conduct instruction.

In discussions about the use of volunteers, it is not uncommon to hear teachers say, "But I wouldn't know what to do with them," or "They're more trouble than they're worth," or "I don't have the time to train them and they really get in my way." On the other hand, in interviews with volunteers used in programs for handicapped students, the volunteers often lament: "I stayed around and didn't do anything all day long." "All I did was change diapers and clean up messes. I would like to do something more constructive than that." "The teacher didn't give me adequate instructions on how to do the task he wanted me to do and became annoyed when I didn't do it properly."

One final question most often asked by teachers contemplating the use of volunteers is "Where do I find them?" The availability of volunteers is quite good in most communities and is limited only by the teacher's imagination. Volunteers can be recruited from a number of sources: community organizations (Jaycees, Women's clubs, etc.), foster grandparent organizations, high schools, grade schools, the P.T.A., and colleges, to name just a few. Usually a phone call and later a personal visit to one of their group meetings will be necessary.

In schools, of course, one must first approach the principal. After the principal gives his or her support, the teacher usually makes a presentation to the student body or to individual classes to recruit volunteers.

In general, the presentation should describe the types of students the volunteers will be working with and what the volunteer will be doing. For teachers with handicapped and nonhandicapped students in the same class, the nonhandicapped students can be used as volunteers, rotating them at least every 5–10 minutes to assure that one student volunteer does not become overly consumed by her task.

Rules for Use of Volunteers

Evidently, using volunteers in the gymnasium can often become a source of displeasure not only for the teacher but for the volunteer. Nevertheless, volunteers can be used effectively with a minimum of friction if we follow certain principles, which we might call "Rules for the Use of Volunteers."

1. Take time to train volunteers.
2. Give volunteers teaching tasks comparable to their levels of training.
3. Establish a system of feedback regarding the adequacy of the volunteer's performance.
4. Establish a simplified, nonverbal system of communication between the teacher and the volunteer.
5. Maintain a system of flexible scheduling of volunteers.

Teachers of the moderately and severely handicapped at Teaching Research have developed techniques for the training and use of volunteers according to these rules. Therefore, let us examine each of them in more depth.

1. Take Time to Train Volunteers

Because volunteers are donating time that is somewhat limited, the available training time is also limited. Therefore, follow a concise and simple method for training volunteers. An initial orientation presentation is necessary in which the teacher explains and demonstrates the volunteer's role in the gymnasium. The presentation should also contain the essentials of behavior modification as required for operating in the gymnasium. More specifically, the following points should be discussed:

1. The role of the volunteer.
2. Overview of the clipboard.
3. The analysis of behavior and the methods used to break complex behaviors into smaller groups.
4. Appropriate cueing.
5. Various types of reinforcement, the necessity for immediate reinforcement, and the principles of pairing social reinforcement with primary reinforcement. Various types of tangible reinforcers should be discussed and described.
6. Correction procedure.
7. Chaining of behaviors, including both forward and reverse chaining.
8. The necessity for record keeping, not for the sake of gathering data for research purposes, but for decision-making purposes in revising programs. Various ways to record data should be described.

Following this presentation, there should be a supervised practicum giving the volunteer further opportunity to develop his skills.

After completing orientation, a volunteer should be able to demonstrate the following:

1. Knowledge of the terminology and principles of behavior modification.
2. The ability to consequate students appropriately.
3. The ability to cue students appropriately in a learning situation.
4. Knowledge of shaping procedures.
5. Knowledge of forward and reverse chaining.
6. The ability to keep records.

The new volunteer is expected to exhibit skills in three major areas of student interaction (i.e., proper use of cues, proper use of consequences, and appropriate data keeping). Additionally, the volunteer must demonstrate a knowledge of the principles of reinforcement, shaping, and chaining.

Later, as the volunteer becomes more proficient, he can be taught additional skills. The following skills can be designated as learning objectives for more experienced volunteers.

1. The ability to analyze a task (i.e., take complex behaviors and divide them into the smaller behaviors that comprise them).
2. The ability to revise program as necessary based on data gathered.
3. The ability to assist teacher in supervision and training of other volunteers and parents.
4. The ability to implement and monitor group activities with a small group of students.

The demonstration portion of the initial orientation session can be conducted by using videotapes or slides. Videotapes of other volunteers working with children or of the instructor working with children can be played and replayed to demonstrate and illustrate points. We consider videotapes a more effective demonstration than the use of live models for two reasons: the interaction of instructor and live pupils cannot be replayed to emphasize or clarify a point with the pupil, and the use of a live pupil does not always allow the demonstration of principles necessary to the instruction. Therefore, videotapes are more suitable for the type of concentrated instruction described here.

It should be emphasized that the instruction is simplistic. Schedules of reinforcement and other sophisticated ramifications of behavior modification are deliberately excluded. If the volunteer understands the basic principles of how to present material to a student, how to consequate the student's responses, and then how to shape and chain responses, the volunteer should be able to perform adequately, provided she works under the supervision of a fully qualified teacher.

The initial orientation session described above consists of only a brief lecture and demonstration; it must therefore be considered nothing more than an introduction to how the students are taught in the gymnasium and to the learning theory used. *The most important part of training is the actual practice of the model with a handicapped student by the volunteer and the feedback that the teacher provides the volunteer following observation.*

Since so much importance is placed on observing the volunteer, a systematic observation procedure is necessary. Though there are many such observation procedures in existence, the one described here has served adequately in many different settings and with a wide variety of students.

Essentially, there are three major elements in observing the effectiveness of the volunteer with the student. The first is the preparation and use of cues and materials; the second is the use of consequences by the volunteer; and the third is the volunteer's ability to record the responses of the student as correct or incorrect.

The volunteer should be placed in a teaching situation with a student and instructed in the use of cues, materials, and reinforcers for the program to be taught. The teacher should demonstrate how the lesson is to be taught; the volunteer should then model the teacher in conducting the lesson. When the volunteer first starts with a student, we recommend that a powerful reinforcer be identified for the student. This will help the volunteer to have a successful first experience working with a handicapped child.

Cue Preparation and Utilization.   The first element of observation made when training volunteers is examining how the volunteer prepares for the lessons to be taught and how that lesson is presented to the student. We call this cue preparation and presentation.

Cue preparation includes ensuring that all materials necessary for the lesson are available and are placed in the most convenient format or position for the teaching of the lesson. It includes the positioning of the data sheet so that the recording process can be facilitated. Once a lesson begins, it should not be interrupted because a volunteer "forgot" some necessary items or materials.

The student's physical deficits must also be considered in cue preparation. What prosthetic or sensory aids need to be provided? As part of the cue preparation, we must consider if the student is wearing the eyeglasses he is supposed to be wearing. Does he have his hearing aid on? Is it tuned properly? Is he wearing the braces he needs? All of these things must be checked before the lesson begins as part of cue preparation.

There are a number of important considerations concerning proper cue presentation for the severely handicapped student. First, pay attention to the sensory deficit some handicapped students possess. If the student is deaf, blind, or both, the manner in which the cue is presented must be modified to accommodate that student. For the student who is deaf, a total communication approach using both signs and verbalizations may comprise the cue. For the blind student, the instructor may have to lead the student through the steps and shape her performance or shape her imitations by touch or a tactile approach. The student with a physical handicap presents other problems, especially in the physical education area. If we say to a physically handicapped student, "Do this," wanting him to imitate us, we must propose a movement that is within his physical capability.

Another dimension of cue presentation is consistency. For the severely handicapped student, consistency of cue preparation is absolutely mandatory. To the severely retarded student, for example, the command "Come here" may sound very different from the command "Come on over here;" consequently, one or the other – preferably the simpler – should be chosen as the consistent command. Instructions in any task have to be consistent, and the amount of consistency necessary is directly related to the severity of the handicap, especially if that handicap is retardation.

Cue presentation becomes very important in any activities that are chained or reverse chained. The task must be presented at the student's present learning stage within that chain. The following example illustrates this.

Suppose the student is learning to strike a ball using a volleyball type swing. She is at a stage where she strikes the ball independently but with the teacher's hand placed at the elbow of the arm supporting the ball. The volunteer must know that the student is to perform the task independently and must provide a support hand on the student's elbow and the command "Strike the ball." However, in preparation for the task, the volunteer may ask, "Do I help the student to do it independently, providing the assistance at the point where the student strikes the ball?" Such decisions can't be left up to the volunteer and must be a part of the cue and program instructions. Without them, the student will be confronted with many inconsistencies in cue presentation that greatly impede the learning process.

Volunteer Observation Form. Figure 7.1 shows the Volunteer Observation Form. Before the program is conducted, the identifying information at the top of the form is completed. "Volunteer" is the person conducting the program. "Observer" is the name of the person observing the program. "Program" is as stated on the Program Cover Sheet. "Student" is the individual who is learning the program. "Date" and "Time" entries are also made.

In addition, prior to being observed, the volunteer is asked to supply the information shown in the center of the form, labeled "Cover Sheet Information." The "cue" is stated on the Program Cover Sheet and should include both verbal and nonverbal cues. The "behavior" is determined by referring to the Phase and Step number on the data sheet and reading the behavior from the task sequence sheet. The "reinforcer" may have been specified by the teacher during the updating process. If so, the volunteer should so state and should specify the schedule of reinforcement. If the reinforcer is not specified, the volunteer should choose the reinforcer to be used from the consequence fille. The "criterion" and "correction" procedure" are stated on the program cover sheet.

The observer records data in the various columns of the form, one tally mark in each of the three sections: cues, consequences, and data. Under the cue section, the following entries are possible:

VOLUNTEER OBSERVATION FORM

Volunteer: _____
Student: _____
Observer: _____
Time: _____ to _____

Date: _____
Program: _____
Cue (Verbal): _____
Cue (Non-Verbal): _____
Student Hand Preference: _____

Correction Procedure: _____
Criterion: _____
Behavior (Phase/Step): _____
Reinforcers: _____

	YES	NO
1. Volunteer has correct materials	☐	☐
2. Materials, volunteer, and data sheet in best position for presentation	☐	☐
3. Student in correct position	☐	☐
4. Student's hearing aid is checked for correct setting before session begins	☐	☐

CUES

Appro-priate	No Cue	Weak	Change Wording	Re-peated

Cues:
Appropriate _____ equals
Total
_____ %

CONSEQUENCES

Positive Reinforcers

Appro-priate	No Re-inforcer	Fail To Pair	Weak	Delayed (2 sec.)	Inappro-priate	Appro-priate

Consequences:
Appropriate _____ equals
Total
_____ %

Correction Procedures & Punishers

Appro-priate	No Cor-rection/Punisher	Delayed	Inappro-priate	No	Cue	Help	Rein-forcer

DATA

	Recorded	
	Correct	Incorrect
Correct		
Incorrect		

Data:
Correct _____ equals
Total
_____ %

Positive Feedback:

1.

2.

3.

4.

Recommendations for Improvement:

1.

2.

3.

4.

Figure 7.1. Volunteer Observation Form.

(a) "Appropriate"—a tally mark is made here if the cue is given clearly and as stated on the Program Cover Sheet; (b) a tally is made under "No Cue" when a verbal cue is not given, when materials aren't presented, or if the cue is incomplete; (c) a mark is made under "Weak" when there is no eye contact, when the cue is not clearly stated or loud enough for the student to hear, or when a verbal cue is given but the nonverbal cue is left out or vice versa; (d) an entry is made under "Changed Wording" when the cue is given clearly but not worded exactly as stated on the Program Cover Sheet; and (e) a tally is made under "Repeated" when the cue is repeated before the behavior occurs, reinforcement is given, or the correction procedure implemented.

The goal is for volunteers to deliver 90 percent appropriate cues on a continuing basis. This goal allows 10 percent error, which may occur across any of the error categories. It has been demonstrated that this goal is obtainable within one week of training for most volunteers. Periodic observations are necessary to ensure that this ratio is maintained.

Consequence Delivery. Since instruction of the severely handicapped is based on the principle that the student learns through feedback, the way the volunteer dispenses consequences (feedback) is critical to the success of the instructional program. Essentially, the volunteer must first be aware of the consequence file that is part of every student's record and is contained on the clipboard (see discussion of the clipboard in Chapter 4). The volunteer must understand the way these reinforcers are prioritized in their strength with the student. Volunteers must understand that they have the choice of these reinforcers, but should the student's performance be poor, it is necessary for the volunteer to choose higher strength reinforcers. With experience volunteers will be able to make more judicious choices of reinforcers, saving the highest strength reinforcers for those times when students are experiencing difficulty with the task or learning environment.

When observing the effectiveness of a volunteer employing consequences with a student, we are concerned with a number of different dimensions. First, is the volunteer giving feedback to the student? Second, is that feedback appropriate? Third, if it is not appropriate, what is wrong with it? The data obtained with the observation form (Figure 7.1) provides answers to these questions.

Whenever the volunteer responds to a behavior emitted by the student, an entry is made under the consequences section of the form shown in Figure 7.1. If the volunteer responds to the student's correct response with a reinforcer that is delivered quickly and with enthusiasm, it is tallied in the "appropriate" column. If part of the reinforcement is primary or tangible, it must be paired with social feedback. If the student provides the wrong answer or does not respond, a four-step correction procedure is initiated; (1) respond "No" or with some other negative verbal feedback, (2) repeat cue, (3) assist the student through the behavior, and (4) socially reinforce. If any of these four elements is missing, an entry is made under the "inappropriate" column of the incorrect correction procedure. The elements of the correction procedure that were missing or delivered inappropriately are also noted. If all elements are conducted correctly, a tally is placed in the column marked "appropriate" under correction.

If the volunteer fails to provide feedback to the student when the student responds, different entries are made. If the feedback would have been a positive reinforcer, a tally is entered under the "no reinforcer" column. If the feedback would have been the correction procedure, an entry is made in the "no correction/punisher" column.

Inappropriate Feedback. If the volunteer gives feedback to the student but it is, in the eyes of the observer, not appropriate feedback, a tally is entered in one of four columns. This is probably the most difficult area for the unskilled observer, and certainly the most difficult area for the volunteer when consequating a student's behavior. Inappropriate feedback comes in a variety of forms.

First, there is what we might term "weak feedback." This is feedback usually given without enthusiasm or given perfunctorily; it is the type of feedback critics of behavior modification frequently observe and make comments about when they say that behavior modification is a mechanistic approach. We see teachers who respond with a repetition of words, "good, good," or "okay, okay," or "all right, all right" with little enthusiasm and little sincerity. To correct this, of course, the teacher must generate some enthusiasm. The personalities of some volunteers make this difficult to correct. In fact, volunteers will occasionally find that they are unable to develop enthusiasm and vary their responses. In those instances it is probably best if the volunteer is given tasks that do not require interaction with the students. A variety of expressions can be used by the practicing teacher or volunteer to overcome the dull, drab repetition of "good," "all right," or "okay." The most common of these is the expression "I like the way you threw that ball, kicked it, moved, etc." or "Good (name task)." Using more enthusiastic expressions like "Neat," "Fantastic," "Wonderful," "Beautiful work," and a variety of sentences that are personally geared to the student will allow the enthusiastic volunteer to relate that sincerity to the student. Another variation of weak feedback occurs when the teacher merely repeats the student's answer. This provides no definitive statement to the student whether his response was correct or incorrect, and without this statement, the feedback occurs when the student fails to respond or responds incorrectly and the volunteer corrects the student while smiling or with an enthusiastic voice, thereby not conveying to the student that the response was incorrect.

The second form of inappropriate feedback is the failure to pair social reinforcement with either primary or other tangible reinforcers. For instance, if the volunteer is reinforcing the student with cereal bits, she must also give a verbal reinforcer as she presents the student the cereal bit. Failure to do so is "failure to pair." This is usually a very easily remedied deficiency and is often prevalent in the new volunteer. A few reminders are usually sufficient to correct it.

A third type of inappropriate feedback is the reinforcement of inappropriate behavior. For instance, a student is told that he gave a right response when he did not give the correct response. This type of error most often happens when a student's behavior is being shaped and the volunteer is to reinforce for less than the totally correct behavior. The tendency of the volunteer, anxious for the success of the student, is to reinforce the student at a performance level less than that required by the program. Inappropriate feedback also occurs when an unnecessary correction procedure was delivered. This situation can arise when the volunteer mistakes a correct response for an incorrect one or delivers the correction procedure before the student has a chance to respond.

A fourth type of inappropriate feedback is that which we refer to as "delayed." Delayed feedback occurs when the student emits a correct response and more than two seconds elapse before the volunteer consequates that response. A delay also occurs if the volunteer waits too long to deliver the correction procedure.

The entire range of observed consequences is recorded on the observation form. The goal is for volunteers to be able to deliver 90 percent appropriate consequences on a continuing basis. This goal allows 10 percent error, which may fall either in the failure to consequate or inappropriate reinforcement areas. It has been demonstrated that this goal is obtainable within a week of training for most volunteers. Periodic observations of the volunteers should be made to ensure that their performance is maintained.

We have found that one of the volunteer's greatest difficulties is to determine what to do when the student responds inappropriately or refuses to respond. The volunteer is often unsure of how to correct the student. In an effort to respond to this difficult area, we expanded the observation form to deal with correction procedures. If one believes that receiving feedback is the way in which a student learns, then the feedback given to a student who makes an error or refuses to respond is important. Further, a precise procedure for correcting such behaviors is needed to provide adequate guidance to volunteers. First, the student is told "No," then she is presented with the cue again and led through the behavior so that she performs it correctly; she is then *socially* reinforced for accomplishing it. After social reinforcement is delivered, the student is once again given the cue to accomplish this behavior. Thus, the correction procedure has these elements, all of which need to be delivered properly: (a) telling the student "No," or "Wrong," (b) readministering the cue, (c) leading the student through the behavior, and (d) socially reinforcing the student. This procedure can be modified for older, more capable students. Whatever modification is made should be consistently applied. If any of these elements is missing, the appropriate notation should be made on the observation form.

Recording Program Data. The third area in which the performance of volunteers is observed and evaluated is their ability to consistently and accurately record data. As mentioned previously, there are essentially only two major types of data recording systems used. The first deals with the standard program data form, and the second deals with behavior problems. Each of these has a separate recording form upon which the teacher should ensure that the volunteer's recordings are correct. This essentially constitutes a reliability check of the volunteer's recording. Is the student being given credit for a correct response when he makes a correct response? Is the recording prompt? Is the recording unobtrusive, that is, not interfering with the conduct of the teaching lesson? As with cue preparation and presentation, the criterion level for data recording is 90 percent correct, allowing a 10 percent error factor.

After observation, the volunteer should receive immediate feedback on his performance. Occasionally, it may be necessary to intervene during an instructional period to advise the volunteer of a correct method of cue presentation, reinforcement delivery, or data recording. Interference with a student's lesson should be kept to a minimum, although for the beginning volunteer, periodic interruptions may be necessary during the first couple of observations.

Thus, the process of training a volunteer consists of delivering a short lecture that includes a demonstration by videotape, modeling for specific lessons, and finally, recording and observing the volunteer's performance in an actual teaching situation.

2. Give Volunteers Teaching Tasks Comparable to Their Levels of Training

Obviously, volunteers, like teachers, have varying levels of abilities, and their effectiveness will be based upon these abilities and their experience. One of the teacher/manager's most important considerations is the assignment of volunteers to teaching tasks that are compatible with their levels of ability.

One of the preferred approaches is to assign a new volunteer an area of responsibility, such as Basic Game Skills or Leisure Time Skills. Usually teachers choose Basic Game Skills. The novice volunteer assigned to teach in this area rotates from student to student, teaching similar tasks—striking, underarm roll, kicking—and through this experience usually becomes proficient in those skill areas.

After demonstrating proficiency in one area of expertise, the volunteer is ready to undertake a second curricular area (e.g., Movement Concepts, General Space). While learning in the second area, she can still be used in the first area with some students, allowing the teacher more flexibility in assigning volunteers.

3. Establish a System of Feedback Regarding the Adequacy of the Volunteer's Performance

Teachers are usually reluctant to observe the volunteer during the first few weeks of training and often reluctant to make critical observations until the volunteer has been in the gymnasium for a few months. Some teachers feel such observations demonstrate a lack of confidence in the volunteer. On the contrary, it is imperative that not only volunteers but also teachers be periodically checked to determine that their interaction skills with students are maintained and that they are presenting materials to the student properly, reinforcing appropriately, and maintaining the data system as required. Without these periodic checks, even the best teacher—and certainly even the best volunteer—will fall into bad habits, become sloppy, and lack precision in teaching techniques. These observations of volunteers should begin when the volunteer first participates in the gymnasium.

Observation of vounteers should be conducted on a regular basis. (The teacher should also encourage the supervisor to observe her as well). The results of the observations should be presented to the volunteers and discussed with them. If available, video equipment should be used to record a volunteer's performance for ten or fifteen minutes and later to play back the videotape, permitting the volunteer to observe himself. The teacher should be present at this reviewing in order to critique the volunteer's performance. If necessary for the volunteer's understanding, the videotape can be played back a second or third time. In giving feedback to a volunteer, remember that the rules of reinforcement apply equally well to the adult as to the student. Volunteers should be reinforced strongly for their good performance areas and emphasis should be on these areas. However, this is not to say that the poor aspects of the volunteer's performance should not be mentioned.

Rules of thumb for delivering feedback.   In delivering feedback to volunteers, you will apply the same principles you have used in changing the behavior of students in your classroom. You will reinforce those behaviors in your volunteer that you have pinpointed as critical to teaching in this educational model (i.e., appropriate cues, consequences, and data collection). Conversely, you will seek to change, through negative feedback, those things your volunteer may do or not do that are inappropriate to this gymnasium model (i.e., repeating cues, failing to reinforce, inconsistency).

You will baseline the delivery of cues, consequences, and data collection. During the baseline observation, you will not deliver feedback within the teaching session. After you have determined the skill level of the volunteer, you will begin the training process, the goal being to raise the volunteer's skill to the established criterion. The process for accomplishing this is the same used in establishing new skills in your gymnasium, using training techniques like modeling, verbal feedback, videotaping, and shaping.

The following rules of thumb have been used by the authors to deliver feedback to volunteers. We are not implying that they represent the only training techniques you should use, or that you will always use them in the suggested order. They do, however, represent an approach to providing feedback to volunteers that has been developed in the training of literally hundreds of teachers.

1. When conducting a baseline observation, wait until the end of the session to give feedback.
2. During nonbaseline, or treatment observations, you should provide immediate feedback if the volunteer makes the same error twice within the same category. Example: If a volunteer repeats a cue, provide feedback immediately.
3. The correction procedure used when two or more errors are made within the same category is as follows:
   a. Your first treatment strategy will be to prompt the volunteer verbally (i.e., "You are changing the cue" or "Don't forget to use social reinforcement at the end of your correction procedure").

   b. You should then mark your observation form with the appro-
      priate mark.
   c. If the volunteer corrects herself on the next trial, you should
      specifically reinforce her for the appropriate response.
   d. Should the volunteer repeat the error, you will then model
      the appropriate response.
   e. Now it is the volunteer's turn again; if she now corrects her-
      self, reinforce her and let her proceed with the program.
   f. If the volunteer again repeats the error, employ an alternate
      procedure. This is essentially the same strategy used when a
      student is failing on a program. The specific branch you use
      will be determined by the type of error the volunteer is mak-
      ing and what you may already know about that volunteer.
      Continued modeling, viewing herself on the video, and ob-
      serving that specific behavior in another volunteer are all vi-
      able training procedures. Another strategy is to have the
      volunteer conduct a simpler program, or work with a more
      compliant student.
4. When delivering feedback after the teaching sessions, you
   should begin your feedback with a minimum of two positive
   statements regarding the volunteer's conduct of the program.
5. In pinpointing weak areas of performance, be specific (i.e.,
   "You are repeating cues," as opposed to "You are having difficulty with cues").
6. If a volunteer "bombs out," give feedback for only one weak
   area. Generally mention the other areas but restrict your comments and treatment to the one area. Remember, we want to
   shape the volunteer's behavior, not make the training so aversive that the volunteer doesn't return the next day!
7. In giving negative feedback, use terms such as "weak area,"
   "something you need to work on," and "problem area" to describe volunteer performance. DO NOT use such terms as
   "wrong," "bad," "poor," "terrible," and so forth to describe their
   performance.
8. You should give the volunteer recommendations for improvement in those areas you pinpoint as weak. If a volunteer has
   done an exceptional job, give recommendations that apply to
   a more sophisticated programmer.
9. There are, of course, exceptions to every rule. Here is one:
   When conducting a treatment observation of a volunteer who
   is in group instruction, we have found it very difficult as well
   as distracting to deliver the correction procedure while they
   are working with the group. We recommend stopping your
   observation after five minutes and pulling the volunteer out

of the activity to give her some preliminary feedback. If there are areas in which two or more errors have been made, start your correction procedure. At the end of another five-minute period of observation, repeat this feedback procedure.

10. Remember, you always have the option of stopping the program if you feel things are out of control.

Videotaping each volunteer should probably occur for fifteen minutes once a month; observations without videotape should be conducted at least once every two weeks. Each observation, with or without videotape, should be followed by a critique. We have found this schedule of observation and feedback to be adequate to maintain the volunteer's performance at the specified criterion levels of 90 percent appropriate cues, 90 percent appropriate consequences, and 90 percent correct data recording.

4. Establish a Simplified Nonverbal System of Communciation Between the Teacher and the Volunteers

One of the often repeated laments of the teacher handling many volunteers is that there is too little time to communciate adequately with them all. Conversely, the volunteer complains that often the teacher does not give complete instructions.

Our model takes that difficulty into account and recommends a system that requires minimal daily personal interaction between the teacher and volunteers, but also provides a system of maximum communication.

The main subjects that need to be communicated between teacher and volunteers are these: The volunteer needs to know which student to work with and when. The volunteer needs to know as much as possible about the student, as much as possible about the program to be administered to the student, the way in which the program is to be administered, what freedom one has with the program, specific peculiarities of a particular program as it relates to a specific student, and the way in which the data are to be recorded.

On the other hand, the teacher needs to know from the volunteer what happened when the student was taught. Was there success or failure? How much success? How bad the failure? Were there any peculiarities about the lesson being taught?

The system recommended herein allows for that communication with a minimum of verbal interaction. The main communication occurs through the documents placed on the clipboard for each student. For this communication to be effective, a prerequisite exists — the volunteer must have been trained in the techniques of teaching a particular type of curriculum lesson. If this training has occurred, the volunteer is ready to focus on a student and the program for that student. The clipboard provides the means for that focus. (See Chapter 4, Gymnasium Management, for a detailed discussion of the clipboard.)

5. Maintain a System of Flexible Scheduling of Volunteers

There are three basic ways of scheduling volunteers. The first pairs a student with a volunteer who conducts all the programs for that student. Second, a volunteer can conduct programs in one curricular area and teach all students or some of the students in that curricular area. The third scheduling system combines these two.

Regardless of which system is used, a volunteer needs to know how much time to spend on a program with a student. This consideration is less critical when one volunteer is assigned to one student and conducts all programs for him during the day. The only timing consideration in this instance will be for the coordination of group activities with individual programs and a concern for conducting all of the programs during the day.

Usually a time schedule that provides guidelines rather than a strict schedule is the best type to adopt. This provides the necessary parameters for the volunteer and yet gives enough flexibility to allow a few additional minutes on a program if the student is not performing well, or less time on a program if the student has performed so well that the volunteer wants to administer a strong reinforcer of additional free time.

The combined system of having some volunteers assigned to areas and others assigned to students allows the teacher to accommodate to both well-trained volunteers and those who are not so well-trained. It also allows the teacher to accommodate to a student who may be having rather severe difficulties but who responds well to one volunteer. For instance, a certain volunteer may be able to handle a student with severe learning problems better than anyone else. Some students with severe learning problems also show responsiveness to few reinforcers; a particular volunteer may "turn the student on" more than any other person. It would be wise, therefore, to schedule that volunteer with that student to maximize the learning possibilities. A new volunteer, on the other hand, should initially be assigned students who are easier to manage.

Volunteer Schedule.   Figure 7.2 is an example of a schedule posted on the bulletin board which has divided the class into time periods and allows for eight volunteers. Scheduling of this type is also valuable when the number of volunteers available may be unknown.

Thus it can be seen that the scheduling of volunteers can be adapted to almost any situation in which the teacher finds herself. If there is a shortage of volunteers, scheduling should be based on priority of student. If volunteers are not well trained, the schedule should assign volunteers to tasks that they can perform; for instance, teaching all or a number of the students in one curriculum area. Finally, if the teacher has a group of well-trained and highly skilled volunteers, she can assign volunteers to individual students and can be assured that those volunteers can run those programs in the order of priority specified for those students. The teacher can communicate the priority programs to be run by circling them on the Program Cover Sheet (see Figure 4.1).

VOLUNTEER SCHEDULE

Time	Volunteer 1	Volunteer 2	Volunteer 3	Volunteer 4	Volunteer 5	Volunteer 6	Volunteer 7	Language Volunteer
8:30-9:00	Jennifer	Alex	Jenny					
9:00-9:30	Alex	Jeff		Valerie			Act. Table	Jennifer
9:30-10:00	Jenny	Jennifer	Alex	Deanna				
10:00-10:30			Jenny	Alex			Jeff	Act. Table
10:30-11:00			Act. Table		Alex	Scott	Valerie	Alex
11:00-11:30			Jenny		Jeff		Act. Table	Valerie
11:30-12:00								
12:00-12:30								
12:30-1:00								

Figure 7.2. Schedule of volunteers.

Small Group Activities $\boxed{8}$

Small group activities for the severely handicapped are considered valuable for several reasons. They provide opportunities for enhancing and generalizing physical education skills learned in a one-to-one setting. For instance, having mastered the underhand roll at a target in a one-to-one setting, it is necessary that the student generalize this skill to group activities that incorporate this skill, such as the elementary game of rolling a ball at milk cartons. In addition, many physical education skills only capable of being taught in a group atmosphere are introduced and programmed here (e.g. sharing, taking turns, and following group directions). The basis of small group learning experiences is still the individualization of cues and consequences as in the volunteer role; but the teacher's task is much more complex in terms of planning the activities and conducting them.

The size of the group is important in order to provide optimum teaching efficiency. Four to six students seems to be an ideal number. This number, of course, depends on the students' developmental age, handicapping condition, and prerequisite skills.

Setting and Materials

Physical education facilities vary extensively from one program to the next, but it is difficult to imagine a setting that could not accommodate the small group activities described here. There are some important considerations to be made when organizing and conducting activity programs for a group of students. A well-lit room with mats on part of the floor would be suitable for most activities. The use of mats or large boxes placed vertically to divide the room into smaller cubicles is necessary for some students. Various shapes should be drawn on the floor (i.e., circles, squares, rectangles, straight and curved lines) to facilitate some of the movement concept programs described in the curriculum. Stools, chairs, benches, desks, and audiovisual aids should be made available for use in the room. Other equipment listed in Chapter 4 should be stored in proximity to the small group area so that it may be quickly obtained.

As indicated in Chapter 3, every effort is made to use reinforcers that are a natural part of the environment. It may occasionally be necessary, however, to use artificial reinforcers to motivate performance in some more severely handicapped students. Therefore, in addition to instructional materials, the teacher may want to include some primary reinforcers and/or favorite toys. This allows the teacher the opportunity to let students engage in favorite activities or play with favorite toys as a reward for working on a "program" activity.

Goals

The following is a list of goals developed for small groups of severely handicapped students participating in physical education activities:

1. Display appropriate social skills in a group setting.
2. Generalize and maintain skills learned in a one-to-one program to a group experience.
3. Respond to nondirective cues.
4. Generalize individual skills into a sequence of skills that later may be incorporated into a game.

A description of how these goals are realized in the gymnasium follows.

Behavior Treatment Programs

The gymnasium is an ideal environment to foster appropriate social behavior useful for both physical education and classroom activities. Acceptable student social behavior for both the classroom and the gymnasium is identified by the physical educator and the classroom teacher. Consistency of behavior treatment programs is essential, regardless of the instructional setting or teacher. Proper procedures are set up to enhance those acceptable behaviors, and a remediation program is established for those that are unacceptable. The physical environment in small groups is an ideal place to target behaviors such as proper interaction in group settings, sharing equipment, taking turns, and helping a friend.

Generalization and Maintenance of Skills

Providing physical education activities that allow opportunities for the handicapped student to generalize and maintain newly acquired skills may be the most important aspect of small group activities. Generalization occurs when a behavior learned in one setting with the particular cue is expressed in a different situation. For example, if a student masters the skill of catching a thrown ball and then learns to catch some other object like a sponge cube, the student has generalized the catching skill. The instructor can assume that the student has learned the skill of catching when he successfully catches various objects over a period of time.

The generalization of skills can be taught in the model classroom through the group prescriptive program. This same procedure can be used in game, exercise, and leisure activities. The first step in group programming is to determine the program content, based on a review of the students' individual clipboards. For instance, all of the students will be working on some basic game and exercise skills, with small groups of students working on similar skills such as kicking and throwing. Therefore, group programs can be established to work on specific skills (e.g., kicking at various skill levels, phases) appropriate to each student. Once a group program skill has been identified, it is necessary to baseline the program using the Group Data Sheet (see Figure 8.1). The baseline procedure used in the group setting is the same as that employed in one-to-one programming. The teacher works independently with each student, but reinforces students who exhibit good group behavior such as observing their peers' performance and waiting patiently. As indicated in Figure 8.1, three students have been baselined on the overhand throw. An analysis of the data indicate that Pam and Matthew need to work on Phase VI, Step 2 and Sue needs additional assistance with Phase VI, Step 1. After baselining and during the scheduled time, the teacher conducts the program, which involves presenting the cues at the skill level appropriate to each student. It is possible at this time to have two students working on catching and one student refining her throwing skill. The number of groups established is left to the discretion of the teacher. A procedure such as this enhances the learning rate for many students because it capitalizes on the use of peer models.

Maintenance of physical education skills already learned in either the one-to-one situation or during group play is a very important aspect of the group activity. This procedure can be facilitated by keeping a list on a chart nearby of the programs each student has completed and including those tasks in the daily activities.

GROUP DATA SHEET

Skill: _Basic Game Skills – Overhand Throw_

Stage: _Baseline_

Names

Pam	Date	3/12/84									
	Phase/Step	VI	2	VI	1	V		IV		III	
	Data	O	O	X	X						
Sue	Date	3/12/84									
	Phase/Step	VI	2	VI	I	V		IV		III	
	Data	O	O	X	O	X	X				
Matthew	Date	3/12/84									
	Phase/Step	VI	2	VI	1	V		IV		III	
	Data	O	X	X	X						
	Date										
	Phase/Step										
	Data										
	Date										
	Phase/Step										
	Data										
	Date										
	Phase/Step										
	Data										
	Date										
	Phase/Step										
	Data										

Figure 8.1. Baseline stage.

Attending to Language

The teacher must be aware of each student's language level. Language used in physical education activities, evoked through the use of cues with students, must be reinforced with a special emphasis on encouragement of spontaneous language during group activities. Generalization of language skills can and will take place during group interaction. Many group activities facilitate a language interaction

among the students that may not be the case in one-to-one programming. This may involve simple responses to questions requiring only
a yes or no. Such interaction may be among students or with the
teacher. In group settings the student will experience many situations where group commands are given and a group response should
follow ("Everybody look over here"). Learning these skills is very important for children who are going to be integrated into the public
school environment. The teacher should continually reinforce those
who respond appropriately and help those with problems to respond
appropriately, and then provide reinforcement.

Making Decisions (Nondirective Cues)

Independent thinking is an important skill for all students to develop. Small group activities give students an opportunity to make
choices and decisions. This skill is developed by teaching students to
respond to nondirective cues. As the name implies, a nondirective
cue provides students the opportunity to make a choice without the
teacher providing direction. Nondirective cues may be used with
either behavior treatment programs or with motor skill programs.
For example, in a small group setting, if John is supposed to be
watching Mary perform a skill but instead is looking at the floor, the
teacher can use a nondirective cue by saying, "John, where are you
supposed to be looking?" The appropriate choice for John to make is
to look at Mary. If John does look at Mary, then the teacher's response should be to provide a mild reinforcement (e.g., "That's right").

Nondirective cues may also be used to help students practice
motor skills. For example, if a student has success throwing a ball
but occasionally fails to step with the correct foot, the teacher, upon
observing the student use the wrong foot, can provide a nondirective
cue by asking, "Which foot do you step with?" If the student responds
appropriately, mild reinforcement (e.g., "You got it") is provided.
However, if the student does not step with the correct foot, a direct
cue (e.g., "Step with your left foot" or "the other foot") must be provided. An incorrect student response at this level requires the teacher
to provide feedback and then model the skill or, if necessary, use
physical assistance.

In small group instructional settings some students perform a skill
independently and correctly for several trials before making an error.
If the error persists, the teacher can move a student from the group
to a one-to-one instructional program by having a volunteer deliver
direct cues and use appropriate consequating procedures until the
student performs the skill successfully and without assistance fro
several trials. The teacher should return the student to the group

setting as soon as the student performs the skill correctly for a specified number of trials.

Scheduling

The teacher must plan well, deciding on weekly programs in advance. The daily small group session should last from 20-30 minutes. This time-frame may be fragmented into any workable units the teacher feels are appropriate. The students' endurance level, strength, and degree of impairment should reflect the amount of time used. The teacher should vary the physical education program from active to quiet activities or to strength or endurance related activities so as not to fatigue the student. Changing from group to individual activities gives variety, but remember that a consistently run program and schedule are better for all involved, including parents, teacher, volunteers, and students. When the weekly program has been established, the teacher must decide how each aspect of the program will be taught and what equipment is required.

Working with Small Groups

After a student has successfully learned a new skill introduced in a one-to-one program, more advanced phases and steps may be taught in a small group environment of initially one teacher to two students, later advancing to one teacher to four and five students. The number of students depends on the levels at which the students perform, the ability of the teacher to manage larger groups, and the availability of volunteers.

Instructional techniques used in the small group setting are nearly identical to those used in one-to-one programming, except for variations in the data collection procedure, the attention given to nonperforming students, and the use of nondirective cues. Probe data, for instance, is only taken on each student over the last two trials for each program. As explained in an earlier chapter, the probe procedure does not employ a correction procedure. Reinforcement is given for successful performance of the behavior. A second difference in group programming is the reinforcement the teacher must give to students who, although not involved in direct instruction, are watching the demonstration and appropriately waiting their turn.

In small group settings, some students may be incorporated into the instructional program as peers and teacher aides. For instance, the group may be learning to roll a ball underhand at the target. A second student, acting as the target, can assist by stopping the ball and returning it to the teacher for the first student's second trial. A student might also be asked to hold a hula hoop while a second student works with the teacher to learn how to move forward, backward, sideways, and through the hoop. In this system, the students alternate as helpers and learners. The helper is reinforced for positive social behavior and good helping.

Small group activities for the severely handicapped may be successfully conducted with one teacher to two students. The addition of more students, however, requires the use of a volunteer. Together, they can teach up to six students. The teacher's role is essentially the same in groups as in one-to-one programming, with changes in the amount of data taken (see Figure 8.2). The volunteer assists in reinforcing good social behavior.

Developmental Stages

Indicated in the following paragraphs are some suggested developmental stages for helping students to progress from individual instruction to group instruction. Not all severely handicapped students will be able to progress to Stage VI. The student should be taken as far as possible consistent with her needs and ability to be successful.

Stage I (Individual)

As described in the previous section, the basic intent of this stage is to ensure that students learn in a systematic way, given that appropriate cues and consequating procedures are used. One teacher or volunteer is necessary for each student.

Stage II (Advanced Individual)

This stage is similar to Stage I but two or three students are assigned to each teacher. Again the attempt is to provide systematic instruction, with the teacher conducting programs, alternating from student to student. This stage allows for early peer interaction, creating opportunities for students to observe the skill performance of others.

Stage III (Transitional)

The ultimate goal of this stage is to advance students from the instructor-directed individual setting, in which specific cues are used, to a generalized instructional format. The students are given general directions and are then assigned an area within the gymnasium to

GROUP DATA SHEET

Skill: ___Kicking___

Stage: ___III___

Names

Matt	Date	11/26/84		11/27/84		11/28/84		
	Phase/Step	VI	1	VI	1	VI	1	
	Data	O	X	O	X			
Mary	Date	11/26/84		11/27/84		11/28/84		
	Phase/Step	VI	1	VI	1	VI	2	
	Data	X	O	X	X			
Francis	Date	11/26/84		11/27/84		11/28/84		
	Phase/Step	VI	1	VI	1	VI	1	
	Data	O	O	X	O			
John	Date	11/26/84		11/27/84		11/28/84		
	Phase/Step	VI	1	VI	1	VI	1	
	Data	X	O	O	X			
Mike	Date	11/26/84		11/27/84		11/28/84		
	Phase/Step	VI	1	VI	1	VI	2	
	Data	O	X	X	X			
	Date							
	Phase/Step							
	Data							
	Date							
	Phase/Step							
	Data							

Figure 8.2.   Stage III (transitional).

practice specific skills. Each student is expected to function independently at the assigned station, with the teacher using nondirective cues and assisted by volunteers providing direct instructional cues when needed.

Stage IV (Peer Interaction)

Stage IV is an advancement over Stage III because at this level students interact with one another through the medium of various skills (i.e., students practice skills together). One student, for instance, may practice rolling a ball while another student practices trapping the ball. The important element in this stage is the emphasis on creating opportunities for peers to interact. If the student performs successfully at this stage, it is possible that later she will be able to participate in some aspects of the regular physical education program.

Stage V (Basic Games)

In this stage, students are provided an opportunity to play basic games using two sequenced skills (e.g., hit and run to first). The fielder in this example fields and then throws to first. Many elementary games can be introduced at this level. The primary point to remember is that no more than two skills should be sequenced. Severely handicapped students need opportunities to learn phases of a game before they are introduced to the complexity of the total activity. Some may never progress beyond learning certain aspects of the game.

Stage VI (Intermediate Games)

This stage is an advancement over Stage V because students are now asked to sequence three skills. A student, for example, might be asked to hit a ball, run to first, and then return to home plate; or to catch a pass, dribble a basketball to the basket, and then shoot the ball. Obviously, sequencing three skills requires not only an advanced skill level but also high receptive and expressive abilities.

The appropriate stage for each student may change from day to day depending on the skill to be learned and the student's ability. It must be emphasized, however, that a severely handicapped student must experience success at Stages I and II before being faced with the challenges inherent in the more advanced stages.

During group programming, data must be maintained to determine the effectiveness of the program. The emphasis on trial-by-trial data found in Stages I and II is replaced in the more advanced stages by taking data only on two of the student's trials. For example, in the Group Data Sheet for five students participating at a Stage III instructional level (Figure 8.2) the students are working on the same motor skill—throwing. It is quite acceptable, however, for the teacher to create situations where students work on different skills, having the students rotate from station to station. In this situation, the teacher has a separate data sheet with the name of each student listed for each specific skill. For the more advanced stages, V and VI, the data sheet is very similar to that used in Stage III except for the name of the program and the identification of the phase. As indicated in Figure 8.3, the students are at Stage V, working on a two-part motor skill sequence, kicking a ball and running to a base, which they have previously learned. The phases and steps of the skills are not identified. The focus of the instruction and, therefore, the data collection is to ensure that the student can sequence the skill, successfully relying on natural cues.

The exact time at which data are taken in group programming depends on the teacher. It is generally recommended, however, that the teacher take data over the last two trials.

The purpose of developing physical education skills is to use them in game or leisure activities. Higher functioning handicapped students who have received one-to-one programming with sufficient op-

GROUP DATA SHEET

Activity: _Kick Ball_

Skill: _Kicking and Running to a Base_

Stage: _V_

Names

Joan	Date	12/1/84							
	Data	O	X						
Harry	Date	12/1/84							
	Data								
Chris	Date	12/1/84							
	Data								
Jon	Date	12/1/84							
	Data								
Aaron	Date	12/1/84							
	Data								
Mary	Date	12/1/84							
	Data								
	Date								
	Data								

Figure 8.3. Stage V (basic games).

portunities to practice these skills in station activities are capable of successfully participating in modified forms of popular games. For instance, students who have mastered the skill of hitting a ball should be challenged to sequence this skill into an activity, Hit and Run, for example, whereby they hit the ball and then run to a base. Only through opportunities like these will students make the transition from successful mastery of an isolated skill to using this skill in a meaningful activity. As students develop more proficiency, teach them more complex forms of various games. This effort, if followed consistently over time, will result in some students successfully participating in regular physical education classes.

Summary

This chapter presented a process for moving severely handicapped students from one-to-one instructional settings to participation in group programs. The focus of the chapter is to ensure that every effort is made to create positive and challenging learning experiences. With good instruction, severely handicapped students will participate successfully in activity programs with their peers. If efforts are made to sequence skills carefully, it is also possible that some severely handicapped youngsters will utilize these skills appropriately in elementary games. This effort, if followed consistently over time, will result in some students successfully participating in regular physical education classes.

Using Medical Support Services 9

The passage of P.L. 94-142 guaranteed that all handicapped children, regardless of the severity of their disability, are entitled to full educational services including physical education. Awareness of this responsibility has caused concern for some physical education service providers. Frequently, one hears the observation that a particular youngster is so severely disabled that he should not participate in physical education activities. While it is true that the severely and profoundly handicapped have a higher incidence of abnormalities requiring medical attention, denial of opportunities to participate in physical education is not only legally wrong, but it also eliminates an educational service that is obviously needed.

Physical education is an educational and not a medical service. Confusion over this distinction sometimes surfaces because of physical education's contribution to physical fitness and thus the area of health. However, as defined by P.L. 94-142, physical educators must also include in their curriculum educational activities that enhance motor fitness, thereby allowing handicapped children to develop important game, dance, and movement skills. The active nature of the physical education environment does pose some concerns, however, which may require the teacher to interact closely with the medical community. Occasionally, the physical education teacher can serve a vital function by detecting physical and movement problems that require medical diagnosis by qualified personnel. Many physicians and therapists recognize today, too, that the educator's observation of how the student moves in the gymnasium may help them understand more clearly the nature of the medical problem.

Services to the severely handicapped require a coordinated multidisciplinary approach to achieve optimum gain for the student. No one discipline can provide all of the needed services. Teachers responsible for physical education can alleviate many of their concerns about liability and safety by interacting with and using services provided by qualified medical personnel. A basic understanding of when and to whom to refer a student is likewise important information.

Therapist Services

Students who are severely handicapped as a result of neurologic and orthopedic impairment frequently require the services of physical and occupational therapists. Therapists share with physical educators a vital interest in the psychomotor domain. While they do not provide physical education instruction, therapists do have an in-depth understanding of normal and abnormal motor development. As a result of their assessment procedures, therapists can help physical educators understand the movement limitations of a particular youngster. Such information can help the teacher avoid the error of physically assisting a youngster to move a limb that is contracted or has nerve damage. Muscular movement that cannot be self-initiated due to nerve or muscle damage requires consultation with a qualified therapist.

Therapist can also provide physical education teachers with pertinent information such as how to lift and transfer a student from a wheelchair to the mat or how to position a severely involved cerebral palsied student. Occasionally, the physical educator may also be asked to do a prescribed exercise program with a student, developed by the therapist. The traditional role of therapists has been direct intervention with individual students. While this may be appropriate for some youngsters, maximum use of therapists' skills today requires that they be available to provide consultant services to educators, particularly those working with the severely and multiply handicapped.

Physician Services

In the past handicapped students were frequently excused from physical education due to a medical waiver. Fortunately, this practice is no longer acceptable because of P.L. 94-142. Physicians and educators alike are pleased to see the elimination of a practice that was frequently abused and misunderstood by many. Recognition that all students, including the severely handicapped, are to receive physical education instruction has necessitated renewed effort to establish effective communication channels between educators and physicians. Most physicians support physical education programs in which the scope and sequence of the curriculum is established. In addition, they feel comfortable with programs that are developmental, task analyzed, and data based.

Within each community, efforts must be made to identify for local physicians the individual responsible for implementing the physical education program for the severely handicapped. A person with appropriate training, professional experience, and empathy toward the severely handicapped will alleviate many doubts that the family physician might have concerning a student's medical safety.

Parents and/or the school nurse play a key role in helping the physical education teacher obtain necessary medical information. Working in the gymnasium with a student who has a congenital heart disorder is imprudent without medical guidelines from a physician. Fortunately, P.L. 94-142 identifies medical services (e.g., consultation with a physician) as a related service that can be provided when necessary. Teachers of physical education should use this option, when necessary, by requesting medical services on the student's individualized education program form.

Support Services

Figure 9.1 is a partial list of what the educator should consider "red flags" and what medical or allied medical services might provide assistance. The left-hand column indicates signs, symptoms, and behaviors which, if evident in a student, may interfere with or prevent his education. While they may be undesirable behaviors, they may not be amenable to behavior modification techniques for their remediation. Examples of such behaviors are physiological conditions like spasticity (stiffness), tongue thrust, seizures, sensory deficiencies, etc.

Certain ethics and laws apply to using professionals. While the ethics are not as binding as laws, failure to respect them may produce a highly embarassing, if not actually harmful, situation.

Legally, referral of a student to medical, paramedical, or other direct care personnel cannot be made without the knowledge and consent of the student's parent or legal guardian. If a problem is uncovered that requires the attention of a physician, the parent should be the one to make the contact.

The following are some ethical considerations for the use of support services: Physicians practicing in a speciality should be contacted by the student's pediatrician, family doctor, or parent. A nurse may see a student for evaluation and/or treatment. Direct referral may be made to speech pathology, visual training, psychology, social work, audiology, and occupational therapy. Any of these individuals may request additional information from the student's physician prior to the delivery of service. If a student is being seen by a professional,

RED FLAGS

IF THE CHILD	SEEK ASSISTANCE FROM
Is excessively stiff or excessively floppy Is diagnosed cerebral palsy	Pediatrician, orthopedist, physical therapist, occupational therapist (through physician)
Jerks, stares, twitches or "blanks out"	Neurologist
Shows decided hand preference before age 3 Has fisted hands Becomes very stiff when attempting to use hands Can't get hand to mouth	Occupational therapist and/or physical therapist (through physician)
If the child has braces, crutches, walker, wheelchair	Orthopedist, physical therapist (through physician)
Is known to be visually impaired Fails to make eye contact Fails to follow object with eyes Fails to focus on objects	Ophthalmologist, visual trainer
Fails to have well-established head control by three months	Physical therapist (through physician), neurologist, ophthalmologist, and/or visual trainer
Does not respond to noise or voice Talks through his nose Is known to be hearing impaired	Audiologist
Has joints that move abnormally Has foot, back, or other obvious deformities Can't spread knees apart 18-24 inches Is very stiff	Orthopedist
Has upper respiratory congestion Is hyperactive or sleepy Has skin rashes Has sores that do not heal Has seizures Has poor hygiene Seems too thin (nutrition)	Nurse
Self-stimulates	Audiologist, ophthalmologist, psychologist
Has normal or borderline I.Q., but is tactilely defensive – severe Has obvious dizziness or balance problems Has trouble in right/left discrimination Has no established hand preference after five years Has severe distractability	Occupational therapy
Has difficulty running short distances without experiencing shortness of breath Has high resting and/or post-mild exercise pulse rate	Nurse, physician

Figure 9.1. "Red flags" indicating the need for support services.

it is considered unethical to request another individual of the same profession to see the student and/or intervene without all parties being aware of the previous involvement.

Consultative Model of Support Services

Most school districts cannot afford these support personnel on a permanent basis. Consequently, specialists who are used frequently can be retained on a consultant basis. For instance, the consulting physical therapist can visit the school one or two times a month. This interaction is sufficient because of the way in which this consultant is used. She diagnoses and prescribes for those students for whom physical therapy has been indicated by a physician. Prescriptions for physical therapy are in programmatic form and the physical education teacher and the parent of the child for whom a prescription has been written are taught by the therapist how to conduct the program. A data system to measure the student's progress through the program is established as part of the data system in the gymnasium. These data and the progress through the program are then shared among the home, school, and physical therapist, and the program is updated in the same manner as the student's other programs. If difficulties in a particular program are manifested before the therapist's next visit, she can be reached by telephone for consultation.

This method of consultation has been used at Teaching Research for the past several years, serving the therapy needs of the students in the center. It has been successful because the consulting specialists have been able to communicate their programs in a sequenced format, have been responsive to data, and have supported the concept that parents and teachers are capable, after instruction by the consultant, of conducting the program prescribed.

Summary

Failure to use available expertise or attempting to fill a role for which one is neither trained nor licensed may well leave the professional open to charges of negligence or malpractice and a subsequent lawsuit. While it is largely the medical field that has been plagued with lawsuits, physical education teachers, as they deal more with severely handicapped students both having serious educational and medical problems, may well be faced with similar difficulties. Using other professionals as consultants is one way to reduce the likelihood of this problem occurring.

Parent Involvement 10

This program summarizes the involvement of parents in the physical education of their handicapped children. It proposes that parents can be involved in three effective ways. The first of these is their input into the development of the individualized education programs for their children. Parents can also be used as volunteers to assist teachers in the gymnasium. The third method of involvement has parents conducting home programs in a system known as the Lunch Box Data System.

Parents and IEPs

P.L. 94-142 guarantees the parents' right to be a part of planning their children's educational programs. Parents, therefore, should help to select and to prioritize the curricular areas in which children should be taught. Because of the requirement placed on educational environments to specify the manner in which the child's progress is measured, by implication parents are required to monitor that progress. In turn, school districts should actively solicit the parents' assistance in developing the individual education program and should welcome parental monitoring of their children's program throughout the school year.

Parents as Volunteers

Parents are perhaps most productive as volunteers, individualizing instruction to children and helping them to accomplish the tasks being taught to them. Volunteers have been found to be especially useful in the teaching of children in the Data Based Classroom by Teaching Research (Fredericks and Staff of the Teaching Research Infant and Child Center, 1982).

The use of volunteers is supported in a study conducted by Fredericks, et al. (1977) which identified indicators of competencies in teachers of the severely handicapped. The primary indicator was the teacher's ability to increase instructional time to the maximum extent. One of the methods of effecting this increase by teachers whose students were making high gains in skill acquisitions was through the use of volunteers.

In discussions about the use of volunteers, it is not uncommon to hear teachers say, "But I wouldn't know what to do with them," "They're more trouble than they're worth," and "I don't have the time to train them; they really get in my way." On the other hand, volunteers used in programs for handicapped children often lament: "I stayed around and didn't do anything all day long," "All I did was change diapers and clean up messes. I would like to do something more constructive than that," and "The teacher didn't give me adequate instructions on how to do the task and became annoyed when I didn't do it properly." Evidently, the use of volunteers in the gymnasium often becomes a source of displeasure not only for the teacher but for the volunteers.

Nevertheless, if certain principles are followed, volunteers can be used effectively both to their satisfaction and also to the teacher's satisfaction. These principles, developed by the Teaching Research Infant and Child Center, are as follows: (a) Take time to train volunteers; (b) give volunteers teaching tasks comparable to their levels of training; (c) establish a system of feedback regarding the adequacy of the volunteer's performance; (d) establish a simplified nonverbal system of communication between the teacher and the volunteer; and (e) maintain a system of flexible scheduling of volunteers. These principles are explained in Chapter 7, Volunteers: Training and Use.

Salient features of effectively using volunteers should be emphasized here. For instance, volunteers can be trained in the course of a two-hour orientation and lecture followed by assignment of roles that allow them to teach a specific skill in the physical education area. In essence, training requires that the volunteer be taught how to cue the child; that is, how to give the child instructions or how to present materials. Second, volunteers must learn how to observe a child's behavior. This observation is facilitated if a detailed task analysis describing the behavior to be emitted by the child is available to the volunteer and has been demonstrated by the teacher. After the child performs the task, the volunteer must provide the child with feedback about the child's performance. Finally, the volunteer must record that performance in a way that can be communicated easily to the teacher.

The above elements require teachers to structure their educational environments so that volunteers have little confusion about what and how to teach the child. The cues, materials, and task sequence for the behavior must be precisely specified. It has been demonstrated that volunteers can be taught to reinforce the child for proper performance but that they have difficulty when the child does not perform or provides the wrong response. This difficulty can be ameliorated by providing the volunteer with a standard correction procedure like the one used in the physical education program conducted by the Oregon State University/Teaching Research staff. The process involves the following elements: (a) Provide feedback (e.g., "No, not quite"); (b) model the skill and recue the student; (c) if necessary, give physical assistance; and (d) provide mild social reinforcement after Step 2 or Step 3. Thus, even if the child does not perform or provides the wrong response, volunteers are comfortable because they know how to respond to the child's behavior. Finally, a precise data system is necessary, allowing the volunteer to record the child's performance on a prescribed form. With these five elements, a volunteer can successfully teach children.

If volunteers are used in this way, teachers will find them to be of much assistance. Moreover, volunteers will maintain interest in volunteering because they will see their usefulness in that they are actually teaching children. Because of the data system involved, they will be able to perceive the children's progress as a result of their teaching. Parents are especially good volunteers in this role and should be encouraged to take part.

There is an ancillary benefit in parents being volunteers in the gymnasium. Because of the instruction they receive as volunteers in how to teach children, they learn skills they can use with their own handicapped children in their home environment. Thus, a dual purpose is achieved by using the parents as volunteers. Not only are parents giving assistance in the gymnasium, but they are learning skills that will enhance the parent's handicapped child.

The Lunch Box Data System

Many parent training models are designed to provide training to parents whose children are not enrolled in a school program. In fact, some educators take the position that if the handicapped child is enrolled in a school program, there is little need for the parents to be trained in the techniques of teaching their own child. Two factors militate against this position. First, evidence indicates that if parents of children enrolled in a school also engage in some teaching of that child, the child's learning will be significantly accelerated (more about this later). Second, pressure from parents who want to participate in teaching their child often requires that they be taught how to teach their child.

Let us consider the latter point first. Our experience is that many parents, especially parents of handicapped children, are interested in doing the most they can for their child and, consequently, are willing to undertake home programs. Moreover, as the success of the school program increases, parents become more eager to help their child. Frequently, they have been discouraged about their child until the school demonstrates some success, at which time the parent's discouragement is replaced by optimism and a desire to contribute to their child's new-found growth pattern. Therefore, as educators, we need to be responsive to the parents' desire and teach them the skills to teach their own child.

But even if the parents were not requesting this type of instruction, it is logical that they be involved in at least some educational activities and training. For instance, it is practically impossible to toilet train a child with only a school training program; a coordinated program between school and home is mandatory if the child is going to be completely dry before reaching the teenage years.

Perhaps even more critical in the child's learning is the acquisition of language skills, which also requires a home/school coordinated program. Language skills—the acquisition of sounds, blends, words, the chaining of words—can all be learned through structured programs, but it is only through the daily use of language, with the child's natural environment responding to his verbalization, that we can hope to make fluent language a part of the handicapped child's repertoire. Since the parents usually constitute a large portion of the child's environment and provide much of the feedback she receives each day, it is necessary for them to be actively engaged in language acquisition with the handicapped child to maximize the rate of acquisition.

Certainly, the entire range of self-help skills requires that the parent become involved in instructing the child. If a teacher is helping a child learn to take off her coat, which she is then required to do in school, it is instructionally self-defeating for the parent to help the child take off her coat to a greater degree than the assistance rendered at school. Each of the self-help skills—dressing, self-feeding, personal hygiene—presents the same situation; therefore, a very closely coordinated program between school and home in the self-help area is required.

Not only in these areas can parents be good teachers, but they can also be effective in any area of instruction. This effectiveness is demonstrated by an acceleration in the rate at which children learn and the quality and quantity of what they learn. In brief, if a parent conducts a daily ten-minute to half-hour systematic training program at home in conjunction with the same training program at school, it has been demonstrated repeatedly that a child will acquire the taught skill in a significantly shorter amount of time. In fact, the data demonstrate that the home/school coordinated program will almost double the rate of acquisition of the skill.

Parents of each child in the program should be approached to conduct at least one home training program. In educational programs comprised of handicapped children, a group meeting should be held with the parents, either as a total group, by classroom, by age group, or by handicapping condition. The purpose of the meeting is to explain home training programs and "sell" the idea to the parents. A major selling argument has been found to be successful. The increased rate at which the child can acquire skills should be demonstrated to the parents by specific examples.

Schedule conferences with the parents to determine which program the parent desires to conduct at home. Great care must be exercised in the initial selection of a program. One of the primary rules is to choose a program that has a high probability of success. If a skill being taught at school is progressing slowly and with difficulty, this skill would not be an appropriate initial selection for a home program. Success will be further guaranteed by breaking the behavior into smaller parts (task analysis) and letting the parent teach one part at a time. Figure 10.1 shows the task analysis for kicking a ball with the preferred foot. This task analysis, of course, is the same one being taught in the school. When this task is being taught to the child, the parent is not faced with having to teach the entire task but only one small step at a time. Thus, the chance for the parent to see some progress is greater and the parent will be reinforced.

After the program has been selected, the parent is ready to be trained. The process of training a parent to conduct programs at home is similar to training volunteers except that in lieu of the initial group meeting with volunteers, the initial meeting with parents is individualized.

Since the same program is being conducted in the home as the school, it is important that this program be coordinated between two environments. Therefore, passing information about the child's progress back and forth between parent and the school on a daily basis is necessary. We have dubbed this daily reporting system the Lunch Box System. The data sheet described in Chapter 6 is the one that is sent back and forth between the school and the home.

The parent will continue to run the program, and data will continue to come back and forth between the school and the home. Fre-

BASIC GAME SKILLS

F. Kicking With the Toe, Preferred Foot

Terminal Objective: Student, from a standing position, will perform a kick by swinging the preferred leg backwards and then forwards, striking the ball with the toe of the foot, causing the ball to roll in the direction of the target.

Prerequisite Skills: Fine Motor Skills — Lower Extremity, K.

Phase I Student, from a standing position, will perform a kick by swinging the preferred leg backwards and then forwards, striking the ball with toe of the foot, causing the ball to roll in the direction of a target placed 5 feet away. The teacher will assist the child by placing her hand on his preferred leg and pushing his leg backwards and then forwards, causing it to strike the ball at the toe of the foot.

Phase II Student, from a standing position, will perform a kick by swinging the preferred leg backwards and then forwards, striking the ball with the toe of the foot, causing the ball to roll in the direction of the target placed 5 feet away. The teacher will assist the child by placing her hand on the child's preferred leg, and forcing the leg backwards and prompting it forwards, allowing the leg to strike the ball on the toe of the foot.

Phase III Student, from a standing position, will perform a kick by swinging the preferred leg backwards and then forward, striking the ball with the toe of the foot, causing the ball to roll in the direction of the target placed 5 feet away. The teacher will assist the student by placing her hand on the preferred leg and forcing the leg backwards, allowing the leg to come forward and strike the ball with the toe.

Phase IV Student, from standing position, will perform a kick by swinging the preferred leg backwards and then forwards, striking the ball with the toe of the foot, causing the ball to roll in the direction of the target placed 5 feet away. The teacher will assist the student by placing her hand on the student's preferred leg and prompting the foot backwards, allowing the leg to then come forward and strike the ball with the toe of the foot.

Phase V Student, from a standing position, will perform a kick by swinging the preferred leg backwards and then forwards, striking the ball with the toe of the foot, causing the ball to roll in the direction of the target.

The following steps apply to Phase V.

Steps:

1. 10'
2. 15'
3. 20'

Suggested Materials: An 8″ diameter rubber ball.

Figure 10.1. Task analysis.

quently, the parent may experience problems. The parent should communicate them as rapidly as possible to the teacher so that the teacher can take remedial action. Frequently, when the parent has such problems, it is necessary to demonstrate how he or she is conducting the program in order to isolate the problem.

Even if the parent is not experiencing problems with the program, periodic conferences—at least once every three or four weeks—are recommended. During these conferences the parent should once again demonstrate how he is conducting the program at home. All teachers begin to acquire some bad habits in their teaching, and parents are not exempt from this fault. This periodic conference serves as a maintenance check on the quality of the home programs. Therefore, the home/school teaching program requires the closest liaison with the parent; daily communication occurs through the Lunch Box Data System, but there also may be a necessity for frequent phone calls and face-to-face interactions at least once a month.

Parents welcome the chance to get together as a group periodically and share their experiences in the teaching of their children. This type of conference is especially valuable for those parents who may be having some difficulties. After listening to how other parents do it, they may be encouraged to try even harder. For parents who are having success, the opportunity to voice that success publicly can be very reinforcing and may help to ensure their continuance in the program.

Children's progress in the home/school program is accelerated beyond what can be achieved in the school alone. Figure 10.2 shows an example of such acceleration. The program shown, modified push-ups, indicates that the child was improving his ability to do modified push-ups by increasing the number he could do at the rate of 1.3 per week when the program was conducted in the school only. When the program was conducted both at home and at school he added three push-ups a week to the number he could do.

Summary

This chapter has described three ways in which parents can be involved in the education of their handicapped children: (a) through recommendations for the child's program in the IEP; (b) through the use of parents as volunteers in their children's programs; and (c) through the use of parents as home teachers in the Lunch Box Data System. Each of these involvements has only one purpose—to enhance the education of the handicapped child.

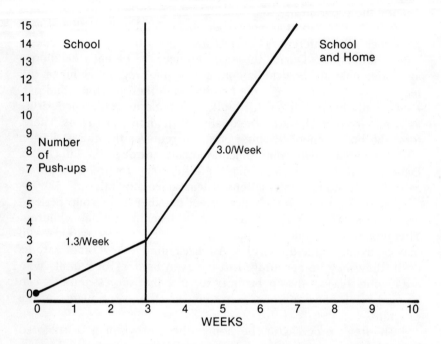

Figure 10.2.   Example of progress of child in a coordinated home/school program.

References

Adkins, J., & Matson, J. (1980). Teaching institutionalized mentally retarded adults socially appropriate leisure skills. *Mental Retardation, 18,* 249-252.

Armstrong, D.G., & Pinney, R.H. (1977). *Record keeping for individualized instructional programs.* Washington, DC: National Education Association.

Azrin, N.H., & Besalel, V.A. (1980). *How to use overcorrection.* Austin, TX: PRO-ED.

Baker, D. (1979). Severely handicapped: Toward an inclusive definition. *AAESPH Review, 4,* 52-65.

Baldwin, V.L., Fredericks, H.D., & Brodsky, G. (1972). *Isn't it time he outgrew this?* Springfield, IL: Charles C Thomas.

Bender, M., & Valletutti, P. (1985). *Teaching the moderately and severely handicapped (Vol. 1).* Austin, TX: PRO-ED.

Bigge, J.L., & O'Donnell, P.A. (1976). *Teaching individuals with physical and multiple disabilities.* Columbus, OH: Charles E. Merrill.

Bijou, S.W., & Baer, D.W. (Eds.). (1966). *Readings in the experimental analysis of child behavior and development.* New York: Appleton-Century-Crofts.

Bleck, E.E., & Nagel, D.A. (1982). *Physically handicapped children: A medical atlas for teachers* (2nd ed.). New York: Grune & Stratton.

Bradley, V.J. (1978). *Deinstitutionalization of developmentally disabled persons.* Baltimore: University Park Press.

Cleland, C.C. (1979). *The profoundly mentally retarded.* Englewood Cliffs, NJ: Prentice-Hall.

Dunn, J.M. (1983). Physical activity for the severely handicapped: Theoretical and practical considerations. In R.L. Eason, T.L. Smith, & F. Caron (Eds.) *Adapted physical activity: From theory to application,* (pp. 63-73). Champaign, IL: Human Kinetics Publishers.

Dunn, J.M., Morehouse, J.W., Anderson, R.B., Fredericks, H.D., Baldwin, V.L., Blair, L., & Moore, W. (1980). *A data based gymnasium: A systematic approach to physical education for the handicapped.* Monmouth, OR: Instructional Development Corporation.

Dunn, J.M., Morehouse, J.W., & Dalke, B. (1979). *Game, exercise, and leisure sport for the severely handicapped.* Corvallis, OR: Oregon State University.

Dunn, J.M., Morehouse, J.W., & Dalke, B. (1980). *Physical education curriculum for the severely and moderately handicapped.* Corvallis, OR: Oregon State University/Monmouth, OR: Teaching Research.

Fait, H.F., & Dunn, J.M. (1984). *Special physical education: Adapted, individualized, developmental* (5th ed.). Philadelphia: Saunders College Publishing.

Federal register. (1977, August 23). Education of handicapped children, Part II, implementation of Part B of the Education of the Handicapped Act. Washington, DC: Department of Health, Education, and Welfare, Office of Education.

Fredericks, H.D., & Staff of the Teaching Research Infant and Child Center. (1982). *A data based classroom for the moderately and severely handicapped* (4th ed.). Monmouth, OR: Teaching Research Publications.

Fredericks, H.D., & the Staff of the Teaching Research Infant and Child Center. (1980). *The Teaching Research curriculum for the moderately and severely handicapped: Gross and fine motor* (2nd ed.). Springfield, IL: Charles C Thomas.

Fredericks, H.D., Makohon, L., Bunse, C., Buckley, J., Alrick, G., Heyer, M., & Samples, B. (1980). *The Teaching Research curriculum for handicapped adolescents and adults: Personal hygiene.* Monmouth, OR: Teaching Research Publications.

Fredericks, H.D., Anderson, R.B., Baldwin, V.L., Grove, D., Moore, W.G., Moore, M., and Beaird, J.H. (1977). *The identification of competencies of teachers of the severely handicapped.* Monmouth, OR: Teaching Research.

Fredericks, H.D., Baldwin, V., Moore, W., Templeman, T., & Anderson, R. (1980). The Teaching Research data based classroom model. *Journal of the Association of the Severely Handicapped, 5,* 211-223.

Gaylord-Ross, R. (1980). Model for treatment of aberrant behavior. In W. Sailor, B. Wilcox, & L. Brown (Eds.), *Methods of instruction for severely handicapped students* 135-158. Baltimore: Paul H. Brookes.

Gearhart, B., & Litton, F. (1979). *The trainable retarded: A foundations approach* (2nd ed.). St. Louis: C.V. Mosby.

Hall, R.V., & Hall, M.C. (1980). *How to use systematic attention and approval.* Austin, TX: PRO-ED.

Hall, R.V., & Hall, M.C. (1980). *How to use time out.* Austin, TX: PRO-ED.

Hall, V. (1971). *Managing behavior part 1, behavior modification: The measurement of behavior.* Austin, TX: PRO-ED.

Hall, V. (1971). *Managing behavior part 2, behavior modification: Basic principles.* Austin, TX: PRO-ED.

Hall, V. (1971). *Managing behavior part 3, behavior modification: Applications in school and home.* Austin, TX: PRO-ED.

Hall, V., & Hall, M.C. (1980). *How to select reinforcers*. Austin, TX: PRO-ED.

Hill, J., Wehman, P., & Horst, G. (1982). Toward generalization of appropriate leisure and social behavior in severely handicapped youth: Pinball machine use. *Journal of Association for the Severely Handicapped, 6*, 38-44.

Hsu, P.Y., & Dunn, J.M. (1984). Comparing reverse and forward chaining instructional methods on a motor task with moderately mentally retarded individuals. *Adapted Physical Activity Quarterly, 1*, 240-246.

Krumboltz, J.D., & Krumboltz, H.B. (1973). *Changing children's behavior*. Englewood Cliffs: Prentice-Hall.

Millenson, J.F. (1967). *Principles of behavioral analysis*. New York: Macmillan.

Mullins, J.B. (1979). *A teacher's guide to management of physically handicapped students*. Springfield, IL: Charles C Thomas.

Panyan, M. (1980). *How to use shaping*. Austin, TX: PRO-ED.

Panyan, M.C. (1975). *Managing behavior part 4, behavior modification: New ways to teach new skills*. Austin, TX: PRO-ED.

Prisbie, R.J., & Brown, P.L. (1977). *Physical education—The behavior modification approach*. Washington, DC: National Education Association.

Sailor, W., Wilcox, B., & Brown, L. (Eds.). (1980). *Methods of instruction for severely handicapped students*. Baltimore: Paul H. Brookes.

Snell, M. (Ed.). (1978). *Systematic instruction of the moderately and severely handicapped*. Columbus, OH: Charles E. Merrill.

Sontag, E., Smith, J., & Sailor, W. (1977). The severely/profoundly handicapped: Who are they? Where are we? *Journal of Special Education, 11*, 5-11.

Ullman, L.P., & Krasner, L. (Eds.). (1965). *Case studies in behavior modification*. New York: Holt, Reinhart, & Winston.

Ulrich, R., Stachnik, T., & Mabry, J. (1974, 1970, 1966). *Control of human behavior, Volumes I, II, and III*. Scott Foresman.

Umbreit, J. (1980). Effects of developmentally sequenced instruction on the rate of skill acquisition of severely handicapped students. *Journal of the Association for the Severely Handicapped, 5*, 121-129.

Valletutti, P.J., & Sims-Tucker, B.M. (Eds.). (1984). *Severely and profoundly handicapped students: Their nature and needs*. Baltimore: Paul H. Brookes.

Van Houten, R. (1980). *How to motivate others through feedback*. Austin, TX: PRO-ED.

Van Houten, R. (1980). *How to use reprimands*. Austin, TX: PRO-ED.

Verhave, T. (1966). *The experimental analysis of behavior*. New York: Appleton-Century-Crofts.

Wambold, C., & Bailey, R. (1977). Improving the leisure-time behaviors of severely/profoundly mentally retarded children through toy play. *AAESPH Review 4*, 237-250.

Wehman, P. (1977). *Helping the mentally retarded acquire play skills: A behavioral approach*. Springfield, OH: Charles C Thomas.

Wheeler, A.H., & Fox, W.L. (1977). *Managing behavior part 5, behavior modification: A teacher's guide to writing instructional objectives*. Austin, TX: PRO-ED.

Williams, W., Hamre-Nietupski, S., Pumpian, I., McDanial-Marx, J., & Wheeler, J. (1978). Teaching social skills. In M.E. Snell (Ed.), *Systematic instruction of the moderately and severely handicapped*, (pp. 281-300). Columbus: Charles E. Merrill.

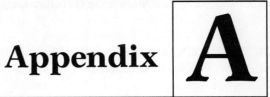

Appendix **A**

Examples from the *Game, Exercise, and Leisure Sport Curriculum*

MOVEMENT CONCEPTS

B. Personal Space–To Execute Various Body Actions While in a Prone Position on Floor

Terminal Objective: Student shall, from a prone position on floor, lie with arms at side, move arms laterally above head, and then curl body by tucking knees to chest and bring arms to chest.

Prerequisite Skills: Gross Motor Skills–Y, QQ.

Phase I   Student shall, from a prone position on floor, lie with arms at side.

Phase II   Student shall, from a prone position on floor with arms at side, move arms laterally above head.

Phase III   Student shall, from a prone position on floor with arms at side, curl body by tucking knees to chest and bring arms to chest.

Phase IV   Student shall, from a prone position on floor, lie with arms at side, move arms laterally above head, pull arms under body and raise self up on elbows, and then curl body by tucking knees to chest.

Illustrations

Phase I   Phase III

Phase II

MOVEMENT CONCEPTS

O. Personal Space – Stand on One Foot – Eyes Open

Terminal Objective: Student stands on one leg with other foot three inches off mat, eyes open, without assistance.

Prerequisite Skills: Standing

Phase I   Student stands between two chairs with both hands on the back of the chair and with left foot three inches off mat, eyes open. Repeat for other side.

Phase II   Student stands between two chairs with both hands on the back of the chair and lifts leg three inches off mat, eyes open. Repeat for other side.

Phase III Student stands between two chairs with four fingers on the back of the chair, left foot three inches off mat, eyes open. Repeat for other side.

Phase IV   Student stands between two chairs with one index and one middle finger on chair, left foot three inches off mat, eyes open. Repeat for other side.

Phase V   Student stands on one leg with other foot three inches off mat, eyes open and without assistance. Repeat for other side.

Phase VI   Student stands on one leg with other foot three inches off mat, eyes open and without assistance. Repeat for other side.

The following steps apply to Phase I-VI.

Steps:

1. Time: 1 second
2. Time: 2 seconds
3. Time: 3 seconds
4. Time: 4 seconds
5. Time: 5 seconds

Suggested Materials: Two chairs

BASIC GAME SKILLS

E. Overhand Strike

Terminal Objective: The student will perform an overhand strike with the preferred arm and hit a volleyball released by the nonpreferred hand just before striking.

Prerequisite Skills: Gross Motor — Lower Extremity, C; Body Orientation, G.

Phase I   Student will perform an overhand strike at an 8" foam ball held by a teacher in front of the student's body at head height.

Phase II   Student will perform an overhand strike with the teacher's hand supporting the student's hand in front of the student's body with the 8" foam ball lying in the student's palm, head height.

Phase III   Student will perform an overhand strike at an 8" foam ball held head high by the student, with the teacher's hand held halfway down the student's arm.

Phase IV   Student will perform an overhand strike with an 8" foam ball held head high with the teacher's hand placed on the student's elbow.

Phase V   Student will perform an overhand strike with a volleyball held head high by the student, no assistance from the teacher.

Phase VI   Student will perform overhand strike with the preferred arm and hit a volleyball released by the nonpreferred hand just before striking.

The following steps apply to Phase VI.

Steps:

1. 8" foam ball
2. 8" rubber ball
3. 8" volleyball

Suggested Materials: An 8" diameter volleyball, rubber ball, and foam ball

Teaching Notes: 1. To perform this behavior, the student should swing the preferred arm backward with a clenched fist and then forward, striking the ball.

PHYSICAL FITNESS

D. Cardio-Respiratory Endurance – Jogging

Terminal Objective: Student runs 300 yards.

Prerequisite Skills: Independent walking; Jogging in place.

Phase I   Student walks forward 25 yards at as rapid a pace as possible. Baseline is determined by averaging 3 trials on 3 consecutive days to get walking rate.

Phase II   Student moves forward 25 yards bearing own weight in jogging posture with arms bent, body leaning forward slightly, and with the heel of each foot striking the ground before the toe.

The following steps apply to Phase II only.

Steps:

1. Reduce baseline time in Phase I (walking) by 10%.
2. Reduce baseline time in Phase I (walking) by 20%.
3. Reduce baseline time in Phase I (walking) by 30%.
4. Reduce baseline time in Phase I (walking) by 40%.
5. Reduce baseline time in Phase I (walking) by 50%.

Phase III   Student jogs 50 yards, no time limit.

Phase IV   Student jogs 100 yards, no time limit.

Phase V   Student jogs 150 yards, no time limit.

Phase VI   Student jogs 200 yards, no time limit.

Phase VII   Student jogs 300 yards.

The following steps apply to Phase VII only.

Steps:

1. Time: 6 minutes
2. Time: 5½ minutes
3. Time: 5 minutes
4. Time: 4½ minutes
5. Time: 4 minutes
6. Time: 3½ minutes
7. Time: 3 minutes

Suggested Materials: Stopwatch

PHYSICAL FITNESS

B. Muscle Strength/Endurance – Carrying Objects

Terminal Objective: Child carries a pail weighing ¼ of own body weight for 6 yards.

Prerequisite Skills: Lifting objects.

Phase I   Child carries an empty pail.

Phase II   Child carries a pail with one cup of sand in it.

Phase III   Child carries a pail with three cups of sand in it.

Phase IV   Child carries a pail with five cups of sand in it.

Phase V   Child carries a pail with seven cups of sand in it.

Phase VI   Child carries a pail with nine cups of sand in it.

Phase VII   Child carries a pail weighing $1/_6$ of own body weight.

Phase VIII   Child carries a pail weighing ¼ of own body weight for 6 yards.

The following steps apply to Phases I-VIII.

Steps:

1. Distance: 1 yard
2. Distance: 2 yards
3. Distance: 3 yards
4. Distance: 4 yards
5. Distance: 5 yards

PHYSICAL FITNESS

B. Flexibility – Toe Touches – Sitting

Terminal Objective: The student, from a long sitting position with arms overhead, bends forward, touching toes, keeping legs straight, and holds for 10 seconds.

Prequisite Skills:

Phase I   The student will sit in the long seated position for 10 seconds.

Phase II   The student, from a long sitting position, reaches forward to knees for 10 seconds.

Phase III   The student, from a long sitting position, reaches forward and touches ankles.

Phase IV   The student, from a long sitting position with arms overhead, bends forward, touching toes, keeping legs straight and holds for 10 seconds.

The following steps apply to Phases I-IV.

Steps:

1. Hold the sitting position for 3 seconds
2. Hold the sitting position for 6 seconds
3. Hold the sitting position for 8 seconds

LEISURE MOVEMENT

F. Swinging

Terminal Objective: The student will get into the swing, propel himself, swing for one minute, and stop himself.

Prerequisite Skills: Extending and tucking the body and maintaining balance while in a seated position.

Phase I   The student will sit in the swing with support from the teacher and with feet touching the ground.

Phase II   The student will sit in the swing with support from the teacher and with feet dangling clear of the ground.

Phase III   The student will sit in the swing with feet dangling clear of the ground.

Phase IV   The student will sit in the swing with feet dangling clear and then the teacher will push the swing forward while supporting the child.

The following steps apply to Phase IV.

Steps:

1. Teacher pushes swing 1 foot forward
2. Teacher pushes swing 2 feet forward
3. Teacher pushes swing 3 feet forward

Phase V   The student will sit in the swing with feet touching the ground and will push himself backwards one push with each foot, picking the feet up by leaning backwards and extending the legs upward, and then swinging forward.

Phase VI   The student will swing forward, and then as the backward swing is initiated, the body will bend forward at a 45 degree lean with the legs tucked under the swing.

Phase VII   The student will swing forward, backward, forward, and then drag feet on the ground during the last backward swing to stop the swing.

Phase VIII The student will get into the swing, propel himself, maintain a swing for 1 minute, then stop the swing and get off.

LEISURE MOVEMENT

L. Roller Skating

Terminal Objective: The student roller-skates to a point 30 feet away, turns around, returns to the designated spot and stops.

Prerequisite Skills: Recognize right and left, put on skates, lace skates, and tie skates.

Phase I   The student shuffles his stocking feet across the floor in a skating fashion.

Phase II   The student wears a carpet square on one foot and slides the foot along the floor.

Phase III   The student wears a carpet square on each foot and slides across the floor in a skating motion.

Phase IV   The student puts one skate on and pushes himself along the floor on the carpet.

Phase V   The student repeats the last phase with the skate on the other foot.

Phase VI   The student uses some support device while moving along the carpet on two skates (chair, walker, helper, bannister, and/or big box with the bottom cut out of it).

Phase VII   The student skates on the floor using the same form of support as listed in Phase VI.

Phase VIII   The student skates on the floor with the assistance of a teacher.

Phase IX   The student skates using the proper skating style and stops when appropriate.

Phase X   The student roller-skates to a point 30 feet away, turns, and returns to the designated spot and stops.

The following steps apply to Phases VI-X.

Steps:

1. 10 feet
2. 15 feet
3. 20 feet
4. 25 feet

Appendix $\boxed{B}$

Clipboard Forms

WEEKLY COVER SHEET

Name: _____

Program	M	T	W	TH	F

Please Note:

LANGUAGE AND CONSEQUENCE FILE SHEET

Child's Name: _____

Reinforcement File

    PRIMARY/TANGIBLE:

SKILLS TO BE GENERALIZED:
(Give the child a chance to show
you these new skills.)

_____

_____

_____

_____

_____

    SOCIAL: (Examples)

Receptive Language

Expressive Language

General Comments

PLACEMENT FORM

For all skills listed below, cue by saying, "Watch me," demonstrate, and then use verbal and/or signed cue listed below.

SKILL	CUE	DATE	Placement Yes/No	DATE	Baseline #/Total	DATE	Posttest #/Total	Comments
B. Underhand Throw	"Throw the ball underhand at the target."				/7		/7	
C. Overhand Throw	"Throw the ball overhand at the target."				/7		/7	
D. Underhand Strike	"Hit the ball underhand."				/7		/7	
E. Overhand Strike	"Hit the ball overhand."				/8		/8	
F. Kicking With the Toe, Preferred Foot	"Kick the ball with your toe."				/7		/7	
G. Kicking With the Toe, Nonpreferred Foot	"Kick the ball with your toe using the other foot."				/7		/7	
H. Kicking With the Instep, Preferred Foot	"Kick the ball with your instep."				/7		/7	
I. Kicking With the Instep, Nonpreferred Foot	"Kick the ball with the instep of your other foot."				/7		/7	
J. Kicking With the Side of the Foot, Preferred Foot	"Kick the ball with the side of your foot."				/7		/7	
K. Kicking With the Side of the Foot, Nonpreferred Foot	"Kick the ball with the side of your other foot."				/7		/7	
L. Trapping or Catching a Rolled Ball	"Stop the ball."				/5		/5	
M. Catching a Bouncing Ball	"Catch the ball."				/5		/5	
N. Catching a Thrown Ball	"Catch the ball."				/14		/14	

BASIC GAME SKILLS

D. Underhand Strike

Terminal Objective: The student will perform an underhand strike with the preferred arm and hit a volleyball which the student is holding with his opposite hand.

Prerequisite Skills: Gross Motor — Lower Extremity, C; Body Orientation, G.

Phase I Student will perform an underhand strike at an 8" foam ball that is held by a teacher in front of the student's body at waist high level.

Phase II Student will perform an underhand strike with the teacher's hand supporting the student's hand in front of the student's body with the 8" foam ball lying in the student's palm, waist high.

Phase III Student will perform an underhand strike at an 8" foam ball which is held waist high by the student with the teacher's hand held halfway down the student's arm.

Phase IV Student will perform an underhand strike with an 8" foam ball placed waist high with the teacher's hand placed on the student's elbow.

Phase V Student will perform an underhand strike with a volleyball held waist high by the student, no assistance from the teacher.

The following steps apply to Phase V.

Steps:
1. 8" foam ball
2. 8" rubber ball
3. 8" volleyball

Suggested Materials: An 8" diameter volleyball, rubber ball, and foam ball

Teaching Notes: 1. To perform this behavior, the student should swing the preferred arm backward with a clenched fist and then forward, striking the ball.

This task analysis should be placed upside down and backwards. This allows the volunteer to review the task analysis, read the program cover sheet, and record the data without flipping pages.

PROGRAM COVER SHEET

Pupil: Date Started: Date Completed:	Program:
Verbal Cue:	Materials:
Instructional Setting:	Reinforcement Procedure:
Correction:	Criterion:

DATA SHEET

Name: _____   Program: _____   X = Correct
                                                        O = Incorrect

| Reinforcer | Phase | Step | Trials | | | | | | | | | | Comments | Date |
			1	2	3	4	5	6	7	8	9	10		

MAINTENANCE FILE

Name _____

PROGRAM:
Terminal Objective:
Cue:
Date Program Completed: _____
Dates to be Probed: _____

PROGRAM:
Terminal Objective:
Cue:
Date Program Completed: _____
Dates to be Probed: _____

PROGRAM:
Terminal Objective:
Cue:
Date Program Completed: _____
Dates to be Probed: _____

Appendix

97 Ways to Say "Very Good"

1. You're on the right track now!
2. You're doing a great job!
3. You did a lot of work today!
4. Now you've figured it out.
5. That's RIGHT!!!
6. Now you've got the hang of it.
7. That's the way!
8. You're really going to town.
9. You're doing fine!
10. Now you have it!
11. Nice going.
12. That's coming along nicely.
13. That's great.
14. You did it that time!
15. GREAT!
16. FANTASTIC!
17. TERRIFIC!
18. Good for you.
19. You outdid yourself today!
20. GOOD WORK!
21. That's better.
22. EXCELLENT!
23. That's a good (boy/girl).
24. Good job, (name of student).
25. That's the best you have ever done.
26. Good going!
27. Keep it up!
28. That's really nice.
29. WOW!
30. Keep up the good work.
31. Much better!
32. Good for you!
33. That's much better!
34. Good thinking!
35. Exactly right!
36. SUPER!
37. You make it look easy.
38. I've never seen anyone do it better.
39. You are doing that much better today.
40. Way to go!
41. Not bad.
42. Superb!
43. You're getting better every day.
44. WONDERFUL!
45. I knew you could do it.
46. Keep working on it; you're getting better.
47. You're doing beautifully.
48. You're really working hard today.
49. That's the way to do it.

50. Keep on trying!
51. THAT'S IT!
52. Nothing can stop you now!
53. You've got it made.
54. You are very good at that.
55. You are learning fast.
56. I'm very proud of you.
57. You certainly did well today.
58. You've just about got it.
59. That's good.
60. I'm happy to see you working like that.
61. I'm proud of the way you worked today.
62. That's the right way to do it.
63. You are really learning a lot.
64. That's better than ever.
65. That's quite an improvement
66. That kind of work makes me very happy.
67. MARVELOUS!
68. PERFECT!
69. That's not half bad!
70. FINE!
71. You've got your brain in gear today.
72. That's IT!
73. You remembered!
74. You figured that out fast.
75. You're really improving.
76. I think you've got it now.
77. Well, look at you go!
78. You've got it down pat.
79. TREMENDOUS!
80. OUTSTANDING!
81. I like that.
82. Couldn't have done it better myself.
83. Now that's what I call a fine job.
84. You did that very well.
85. Congratulations!
86. That was first-class work.
87. Right on!
88. SENSATIONAL!
89. That's the best ever.
90. Good remembering!
91. You haven't missed a thing.
92. It's a pleasure to teach when you work like that.
93. You really make my job fun.
94. Congratulations. You got (# of behavior) right.
95. You've just about mastered that!
96. One more time and you'll have it.
97. You must have been practicing.

Appendix  D

40 Ways to Deliver a Nondirective Verbal Cue

1. What do you do next?
2. Look carefully.
3. Think carefully.
4. Is that right?
5. What do you think about the (*name of item*)?
6. What do you need to get?
7. Where do you need to work?
8. Where do you need to look?
9. Where do you need to go?
10. What do you need to do with the (*name of item, e.g., ball*)?
11. What else do you need to do?
12. Is that all?
13. Is there more to do?
14. Go ahead.
15. Where else do you need to (*name of activity, e.g., run*)?
16. What do you do to (*name of activity, e.g., run the bases*)?
17. How are you going to (*name of activity, e.g., serve the ball*)?
18. What do you need to do first before you can (*name of activity, e.g., catch the ball*)?
19. What do you need to do after you (*name of activity, e.g., catch the ball*)?
20. Where do you need to (*name of activity, e.g., stand to kick the ball*)?
21. You know what to do now.
22. Is that all you need to (*name of activity, e.g., do when you field the ball*)?
23. What are you going to do about (*name of item or problem, e.g., missing the ball*)?

24. There seems to be a problem with the (*name of item, e.g., equipment*).
25. What do you need to say?
26. What can you tell (*name of person*) about (*name of activity or time period, e.g., your softball game or how long it took you to run the 100-yard dash*).
27. What did I ask you to do?
28. What's the last thing you need to do?
29. What's the first thing you need to do?
30. What do you do when you hear (*name of sound, e.g., the gun sound*)?
31. Look carefully at (*name of item or location, e.g., where the players are standing*).
32. You have something to do.
33. You are not done yet.
34. Think carefully about what you need to do next.
35. How can you make it easier to (*name of activity, e.g., catch the ball*)?
36. What do you say (*or do*) when that happens?
37. How are people going to (*name of activity, e.g., play frisbee*)?
38. What do you need to do when you (*name an object or condition, e.g., the runner kick the ball and run to first*)?
39. What do you need to do when you feel (*name of condition or item, e.g., you are out of breath*)?
40. What do you need to look for?

Glossary

aggressive behavior – an inappropriate physical or verbal behavior that directly affects another individual.

baseline – the process used to specifically pinpoint where a student is within a particular skill prior to instruction.

behavior – any observable and/or measurable action.

behavior modification – systematic use of cues and consequences to strengthen or diminish social and motor behaviors.

behavioral objective – a specific goal defined in terms of observable and measurable actions.

bracketing – the process incorporated into the baseline procedures to facilitate the movement back through the task analysis when the child performs poorly.

branching – the adding of steps to make the increment easier from one phase of the program to the next phase.

clipboard – the device allowing an independent and systematic approach to communication between the teacher and volunteers. It contains all the directions for running programs as well as information regarding the student's learning capabilities.

consequence – feedback immediately following a behavior that increases or decreases a behavior's occurrence.

contingency cue – student's choice of what to do once the original task is cued and then completed.

cooperative play – children using the same toys or engaging in the same activities and exhibiting some interaction.

correction procedure – a portion of the instructional model that gives the student assistance when experiencing difficulty in learning a motor skill.

cover sheet – a listing of the programs presently being conducted with the student that informs the volunteers of the priority programs for the day.

criterion – level of acceptable performance of a behavior involving rate, time, distance, etc.

cue – signal, request, or condition that does or can be made to influence the occurrences of a behavior.

Data Based Gymnasium Model–a prescriptive physical activity program for students whereby decisions are based upon the student performance data.

data sheet – a form that contains all of the data points.

delayed cue–too long a time lapse between initiation of the program and the cue.

delayed reinforcer–a delay of more than two seconds between the successful performance of a task and feedback.

enabling behaviors–a series of behaviors listed in a sequential order that make skills less difficult and easier to learn.

environmental cue–a natural cue inherent in the game as it is played (e.g., a fly ball hit to the left fielder).

expressive language level–the degree of language that the student is able to emit.

fading–the gradual elimination of reinforcers or cues.

feedback–a consequence given immediately after a child responds to the cue. Consequences can be verbal, gestural, and/or physical.

forward chain–a sequence of enabling behaviors that make up a terminal behavior and are taught in the order in which they occur.

functional reinforcers–those reinforcers that relate specifically to the skill being taught (e.g., the student was successful in propelling himself on the swing, so the teacher lets him swing).

Game, Exercise, and Leisure Sport Curriculum–a series of physical education task analyses developed as a result of a cooperative effort between Oregon State University and Teaching Research.

generalization–effect occurring when the student learns a skill in a one-to-one instructional setting and can perform the skill in a group activity (e.g., using the skill of kicking in a kickball game).

generalized reinforcer–points or tokens the student receives, that can be traded at a specified time for such things as food, free time, choice time, and/or time with a special friend or activity.

Individualized Educational Program (IEP)–a written plan developed for a student that includes educational goals and objectives jointly developed by parents and school officials.

least restrictive environment (LRE)–an educational placement that maximizes the student's potential to learn and is based upon the student's ability to learn.

maintenance–a periodic check of skill retention.

modeling–observing the teacher, volunteer, or aide perform a skill prior to being cued.

multidisciplinary approach–various disciplines working together to provide the student an appropriate educational experience.

noncompliant behavior–behavior occurring when a student either chooses not to perform the task at all or performs the skill very poorly, sloppily, or incompletely.

noncumulative skill—type of skill in which the steps being taught are not directly related to each other in a forward chain sequence.

nondirective cue—cueing process that gives the student an opportunity to think about the appropriate response without giving any idea as to what is expected (e.g., "Johnny, what should you do when you hit the ball?").

nonverbal cues—cues that provide information to the student in a nonverbal manner (e.g., teacher glance).

paired reinforcement—term used for the pairing of a social reinforcer with a tangible reinforcer.

phases—a series of enabling behaviors sequenced in a manner that eventually lead to the successful completion of the terminal objective.

physical assistance—the physical manipulation of the student through a movement sequence.

placement—the initial testing procedure designed to determine which skills the student can or cannot perform.

positive reinforcer—any consequence that increases or strengthens a behavior.

posttest—test given after the final phase and/or step has been learned to determine if the skill has been retained.

prerequisite skill—entry level skills needed prior to learning a new objective.

prescriptive program—an individualized program that is systematically structured to allow for the collection of necessary data.

primary reinforcer—reinforcers that satisfy certain biological needs such as eating, drinking, and which are not learned.

probe—periodic check in data collection to validate progress of a student.

probe ahead—the process used to maximize the student's movement forward through a program.

probe back—the process used to see if a previous phase has been retained when a student experiences difficulty at a particular phase.

probe data—the data-keeping process used during group instruction whereby two data points are recorded at the completion of the lesson.

prompt—a form of physical assistance whereby the instructor lightly touches the student to initiate the appropriate motor response.

punishment—a consequence delivered immediately following a behavior to decrease the probability of the behavior recurring.

receptive language level – the degree of understanding that the student is able to process.

reinforcer – anything pleasurable that increases the probability of the behavior recurring.

reverse chain – technique whereby the student is assisted with the initial phases of the motor skill and is allowed to complete the final phases independently.

self-indulgent behavior – includes tantrumming, crying, pouting, sulking, screaming, and making other noises. These behaviors are ignored and the student is reinforced when the behavior stops.

self-reinforcers – reinforcers that are internalized.

self-stimulatory behavior – includes filtering, rocking, playing with body parts, and self-destructive behaviors that cause damage to the student. These behaviors should be restrained and the student should be reinforced immediately when they stop.

shaping – a process whereby the student is reinforced for behaviors that are approximations of the desired skill.

social reinforcers – words, physical contact, or learned reinforcers that are not related to biological needs. They inform the student that the behavior was appropriate.

steps – further breakdown of a phase that may be represented by distances, times, and/or number of repetitions.

tangible reinforcers – includes such things as food, water, juice, toys, time on the playground, viewing television, or any item or activity that the student enjoys.

task analysis – the breaking down of a skill into smaller sequentially ordered phases and steps that facilitate the student's ability to achieve.

terminal objective – the targeted motor skill for each task analysis.

time out – refers to a behavior modification procedure in which a student is removed from a setting for a specified period of time following an inappropriate behavior and placed in a "neutral" environment.

token economy – a reinforcement system set up in which tangible objects are used as reinforcers to be later exchanged for desired objects or activity.

total task – condition in which all parts of the skill are sequentially performed during each trial and assistance is given whenever needed throughout the sequence of parts.

update – the process whereby the teacher prepares the student's clipboard for the next day by making the necessary alterations in the program (e.g., cues, consequences and/or reinforcers).

volunteer observation form – the form used by the teacher to make observations on the volunteers as they conduct one-to-one instruction with the students.

volunteer – an assistant who provides one-to-one instruction with the student.

weak cue – a cue given to the student that is of insufficient strength to elicit the desired response.

weak feedback – feedback given without enthusiasm or given perfunctorily.

weekly cover sheet – see cover sheet.